T0095651

Back Home to
MONTANA

Sally Campbell Repass

authorHOUSE®

AuthorHouse™
1663 Liberty Drive
Bloomington, IN 47403
www.authorhouse.com
Phone: 1-800-839-8640

Published by AuthorHouse 10/4/12

ISBN: 978-1-4772-7744-7 (sc)
ISBN: 978-1-4772-7743-0 (e)

Acknowledgement

Talent: Tracy Fisher
Represented by: East Coast Talent (GA)
Agent: Barbara Garvey
Address: 3 Central Plaza Rome, Georgia 30161-3233 United States

Phone: (404) 660-7709
Email: ectagency@gmail.com
Website: http://www.ectagency.com/

Photograph taken on the set of: Bethlehem

Film synopsis:

"A dramatic story of lies and manipulation set in a small Southern town. The film follows the life of a working-class, single father, Joseph. He turns to his faith to find guidance for his life, becoming an example to his co-worker and friend Robbie. His faith is made stronger through struggle with his rebellious runaway daughter, Rebecca. He finds her uncontrollable and disciplines her with beatings, hoping that she will make a turn for the better. However, in Rebecca's heart hate grows towards her father and she desires for revenge. She conspires a plan to destroy his life through lies and trickery."

Director: Alex Zhuravlov
Photographer: Joe McDonough
Produced by: Holy Color Films

Contents

Chapter 1

Dr. Miranda Sterling left her home on the Parker Ranch in Laurel, Montana and moved to Prince Edward Island to become partners with Dr. Laura Fisher at PETS PARADISE CLINIC. She had such a love for animals and even adopted six Siberian Huskies which she housed at her quaint little home in the country. Life was good. She made lots of new friends, both girls and guys. Little did she know that one of the guys would one day become her husband.

She had always been an animal lover, even when she was a child. Not long after she moved to Prince Edward Island someone back in the states gave her a Husky dog. She was so excited but had to keep her at the clinic until she could get a dog lot fenced in for Saber Moon. Laura told Miranda that her boyfriend, Shan, had a friend named Mardi Carson, who was a good carpenter and would probably do the work for her. The first time she saw him she was in awe of his good looks. She was even more excited to see that he was not wearing a wedding band.

Things worked out extremely well for Mardi and her. They were planning a double wedding with Laura and Shan. Miranda's family flew to Prince Edward Island for the wedding. They all came except Miranda's mother, Rachel, who passed away several years ago due to ovarian cancer. Miranda missed her mother very much and knew she always would. She was so thankful to still have her dad, Grayson Sterling.

Her brother, Rob, married Kati Campbell from the island and moved there. Miranda was so happy things were working out for Rob. He had been through a traumatic time with his former girlfriend, who was a psychopath. Little did he know when he asked her to marry him that his life would be in excessive danger. She was extremely jealous and tenacious when it came to Rob. She would stalk him day after day. Finally, she chose her time and broke into his apartment. She was lurking in the shadows when he entered the front door. She instantly raised the gun and shot him.

After working on Prince Edward Island for awhile, Miranda felt it was time to go back home to Montana. Arrangements were made and she and Mardi made the move. They had only been back home on the ranch for six months when her dad passed away. She had been the one to find him early one morning when he never came down to breakfast. He had passed away sometime during the night. It was such a shock to all the family, since he hadn't been physically sick. Since the death of his grandson, Isac, he had never been the same. He blamed himself for Isac's death and really never got over it. He was laid to rest beside his beautiful wife, Rachel, in the Parker Family Cemetery on the ranch.

Miranda relived that morning over and over in her mind. She could still see her dad as he lay there in his bed, so cold and still. Many nights she had nightmares about him. She would wake up in a cold sweat with her heart pounding. She prayed these nightmares would soon be over. They were taking a toll on her. She was feeling so tired lately and it was beginning to show in her face. Mardi was so worried about her.

Miranda was so glad she and Mardi had made the move back to the ranch. She was very thankful for the time she had with her Dad the last six months of his life.

One morning after another terrible nightmare, Mardi decided he had to take control.

"Miranda, Darling...I think you need to see a doctor."

She looked at him with fear in her eyes, "Jennifer's a doctor. She can help me."

"I'm not talking about a medical doctor," said Mardi softly.

"Do you mean a shrink?" she asked agitated.

"I mean a Psychiatrist."

"Do you think I'm crazy?" she asked angrily.

"No, I don't think you're crazy. I do think you need some help dealing with these continuing nightmares."

"I don't think a shrink can help me!"

"Please, Miranda...just talk to one. It is killing me to see you this way."

"What do you think it is doing to me, Mardi?" she asked in a cold voice.

Seeing the icy stare in her eyes he replied, "I can see what it's doing to you, my dear."

"You just don't understand what I'm going through!" she exclaimed in a shrill tone.

"I'm sorry, Miranda. No, I don't understand what you are going through. I just want to help you, because I love you so much."

"I know..." she responded." I'm sorry Mardi!"

"Will you go to see a doctor? I'm sure Jennifer would know a good one."

"Okay, I will talk to her and see what she has to say."

"Good. Thank you, Miranda. I just want what's best for you. I think you know that."

"I do know, Mardi. Thank you for caring so much!" she exclaimed as she went into his arms.

"You're welcome, my love. For you, I would do anything!"

"I know that, Mardi! I would do anything for you also!"

"Why don't you talk to Jennifer and ask her to recommend a good doctor? I'm sure she knows one."

"I'll do that…I promise. I'll talk to her when she comes home tonight."

Jennifer arrived home from work around five-thirty. Miranda had dinner ready and they all sat down to eat. Conversation was minimal. Miranda was quiet and ate very little. She caught Mardi looking at her several times and she knew what was on his mind. She would speak to Jennifer as they were cleaning up the kitchen. Although she hated to admit it, she knew she needed help in dealing with the nightmares she was having almost every night.

Miranda and Jennifer cleared the table and carried the food and dishes into the kitchen. Miranda decided now was as good a time as any. "Jennifer, I have something I need to talk over with you."

"Sure, Miranda. What is it?"

"As you know, I keep having recurring nightmares about Dad dying and finding him in his bed. I thought I would get over it, but they occur almost every night. It's wearing me down and I don't know how much longer I can cope."

"I'm sorry to hear that, Miranda!" exclaimed Jennifer.

"Mardi made me promise to talk to you and ask you to find a good psychiatrist for me to talk to. He thinks I need help dealing with the situation."

"It surely won't hurt to talk to someone. I will inquire

tomorrow at work and should have a name for you when I get back home."

"Oh, thank you, Jennifer," she said giving her sister a hug.

"You're welcome, my dear. Anyway, what are sisters for?" she asked with a smile as she hugged Miranda tightly.

Miranda lay her head on Jennifer's shoulder and the tears started. It was like a dam had burst. Miranda sobbed and sobbed. Jennifer held her and tried to comfort her, as she cried along with her. They cried for all the loved ones they had lost. Not only their parents, Grayson and Rachel, but also little Isac, Jennifer's son. All the memories came flooding back and tears were the only relief for the sisters. Jennifer knew she had to be strong for Miranda. That's how sisters are. It was hard giving up her parents, but unless you've lost a child, NO ONE knows the pain you go through. When little Isac died, she wanted to die too! She knew she couldn't give up though, because she had her wonderful husband, Gabe, and also still had Isabelle to raise. Isabelle missed her twin brother very much.

After awhile the sisters parted and dried their eyes. Each one thanked the other for being there for them. Miranda was so thankful to be home with her family! They finished in the kitchen and went to the den where Gabe and Mardi were watching TV. Mardi looked up at Miranda and gave her a smile. Somehow he knew she had talked to Jennifer and he felt a sigh of relief. He loved that girl so much and worried when anything hurt her. He had been praying for her, too.

"Come join us," said Gabe giving the girls a smile. "We'll even turn off the TV and talk to you."

"How noble of you," said Jennifer smiling.

"Of course you know we are the best!" he exclaimed with a laugh.

"Of course you are," said Jennifer with a chuckle. "You don't think we would have married you if you weren't, do you?"

"I don't think so, do you Mardi?" he asked looking straight at Mardi for an answer.

"No, our wives are very smart. They know the BEST when they see it," chuckled Mardi.

"That's enough bragging guys," said Jennifer rolling her eyes at her husband.

"We're finished," laughed Gabe. Changing the subject he asked, "So, how was your day at work, Jennifer?"

"It was very busy. Actually I had an overload of patients today. Dr. Dane Campbell was sick and we had to work in his patients."

"I'm sure that was rough," said Miranda.

"Yes, it was. Days like this are hard and makes you wish you had chosen another profession."

"Hopefully he will be back tomorrow," added Miranda.

"I sure hope so," said Jennifer with a yawn.

Chapter 2

Work was easier for Jennifer the next day. Dr. Campbell was back to work and feeling better. Jennifer sure was glad for that. Since he had been there much longer than she had, she decided to ask him to refer a good psychiatrist for Miranda. She asked him to come to her office after closing time. At five o'clock sharp the door to her office opened and he walked in.

"Come in, Dane," said Jennifer with a smile. "Thanks for taking time to see me."

"You're very welcome, Jennifer. What can I help you with?"

"I need for you to recommend a good psychiatrist."

"For you?" he asked in surprise.

"No," she laughed. "I think I'm still sane."

"I didn't mean that you weren't."

"I know...I was just kidding. Actually, my sister Miranda has been having a hard time coping with our Dad's death."

"I'm sorry to hear that, Jennifer."

"I think she really needs someone to talk to besides the family. That's why I wanted to find a good psychiatrist for her. She has nightmares almost every night and they are always the same. She was the one to find Dad. He died in his sleep."

"Oh, that has to be rough!"

"Yes, it is...especially since she is having recurring nightmares about it. She wakes up screaming and her heart pounding. I am very worried about her. She is losing weight from not eating and sleeping."

"I can understand that. I know a couple good doctors that might be able to help her. The one I would recommend is Dr. Garth Sable."

"I think I have heard of him, but don't know anything about him."

"In my book, he is the best."

"What age is he?" asked Jennifer.

"He's young, probably around thirty-five."

"That's good. Is it hard to get an appointment with him?"

"I'll give him a call and tell him you will be calling."

"Thanks, Dane. I really appreciate your help."

"You're welcome, Jennifer. What are friends for?"

"Thanks for being my friend," she said with a smile.

"My pleasure," he replied as he got up and walked out the door.

Jennifer was happy to have a name to give Miranda when she got home that night. She also had made an appointment for her which would be in three days. She felt sure getting an appointment so soon was due to Dr. Campbell talking to Dr. Sable. It's good to have connections, she thought. She truly hoped this doctor could help Miranda. She needed to get her life back. She could see the strain it was causing in her marriage to Mardi. He was so worried about his wife. Miranda had become withdrawn and talked very little to any of her family, including her husband.

The day passed quickly and soon Jennifer arrived home. Miranda was in the kitchen cooking dinner. This was a surprise...

"Hello, Miranda!" exclaimed Jennifer as she walked in the door. "It's good to see you up and about. Something sure smells good."

"Thank you, Jennifer. I decided I should get out of bed and try to be productive."

"Great! I have some good news for you. I found you a doctor and got you an appointment this week. His name is Dr. Garth Sable. Dr. Campbell recommended him very highly."

"Thank you, Jennifer. Do you think you could go with me?"

"I think that could be arranged, if that is what you truly want."

"It is...I don't want to go alone!"

"What about Mardi?" asked Jennifer.

"No, I would rather you go with me."

"Okay, I will rearrange my schedule so that I can go."

"Oh, thank you, Jennifer!" exclaimed Miranda. "You are a dear sister!"

"You know I love you, Miranda and would do anything to help you."

"I'd better finish getting dinner ready," said Miranda changing the subject.

"Give me a minute and I will help you," said Jennifer.

"Thank you," said Miranda.

The girls worked together and put a delicious meal on the table. They could tell Mardi and Gabe really enjoyed it. It was good to sit there together, eating and talking. Jennifer observed Miranda and saw that she was very quiet and ate very little. She was looking very pale and fragile. She had lost weight and her clothes just hung on her. Jennifer was worried about her. She sure hoped Dr. Sable could help her. She also thought Miranda needed to go to a medical doctor, which she was going to suggest, as soon as this other appointment was over. Hopefully she would be willing to go see Dr. Campbell. He was her choice of the two doctors she worked with.

Three days later, Miranda, dressed in a beautiful emerald green silk blouse, cream colored pants and matching high heels, was ready for her doctor appointment. Jennifer was dressed in a royal blue silk blouse and black pants. Both girls looked stunning, even though Miranda was still looking somewhat tired. Earlier, she had looked into the gilded leaf mirror and saw the dark circles under her eyes. She knew she needed help. She was so thankful for her sister who was willing to help her get better.

They left the house thirty minutes before the appointment time. Miranda was quiet on the drive over to Billings. Jennifer never tried to start a conversation with her. Sometimes silence is best.

Fifteen minutes later they arrived at Dr. Garth Sable's office. Jennifer could tell that Miranda was somewhat nervous. "Everything will be okay, Miranda," reassured Jennifer.

"I hope so. I really hope he can help me get over these nightmares," replied Miranda.

"This is a start at least. With prayer and Dr. Sable's help, I think you will get well soon."

"I hope you're right," sighed Miranda.

The two girls walked into the office and went to the reception window. Jennifer told the girl behind the window that Miranda was there to see Dr. Sable. They were asked to have a seat and fill out some papers, since this was Miranda's first visit.

Miranda was called in about twenty minutes past her

appointment time. She turned to her sister and asked, "Will you go with me, Jennifer?"

"Of course I will," replied Jennifer. So both of them followed the nurse into a room where Dr. Sable was sitting at his desk.

"Hello ladies," said Dr. Sable in a pleasant voice as he rose to his feet. "How may I help you?"

"I brought my sister to talk with you, Dr. Sable. She has been having recurring nightmares since our dad died a few months ago. She was the one who found him. He died in his sleep. She just can't seem to get past this."

Dr. Sable looked at Miranda and smiled. She gave a faint smile back. "Miranda, tell me about the nightmares."

"I hardly know where to start," she replied looking nervous.

"Suppose you start at the time of your dad's death. I know this will be painful, but I think it is necessary."

"Okay, I'll try..."

Miranda told him about her dad and how she and Mardi had moved back to the ranch to be with him. She was very close to him and it was such a shock when she found him dead. She told Dr. Sable about the recurring nightmares and about finding her dad after he had died. She went into detail about how it affected her and was crying as she talked. Dr. Sable listened intently while she talked and cried. He knew this was good therapy for her... to get it out in the open. Tears bring relief, so he let her cry. By the time their session was over, Miranda had stopped crying.

"How do you feel, Miranda?" asked Dr. Sable.

"Honestly, I feel better."

"That's good!" he exclaimed. "I would like to see you

a couple times a week for awhile. I honestly think we can get through this together."

"Okay, I'm sure you know best."

Jennifer sat there the whole time and never said a word. She was wiping tears from her own eyes. The girls got up to leave, and Miranda thanked Dr. Sable for seeing her.

"You're welcome, Miranda. Thank you for trusting me enough to share this with me. I really think we will make a break-through soon."

He looked at Jennifer and thanked her for bringing her sister to see him. Jennifer gave him a smile and said, "You're welcome."

"See you in three days Miranda," reminded Dr. Sable.

"I'll be here," she answered.

The girls left and headed back to the ranch. Miranda was quiet on the ride back, except for thanking Jennifer for taking her. As they pulled into the driveway at the house, Jennifer decided to ask her a question. "How did you like Dr. Sable?"

"I think he is very nice," replied Miranda.

"Do you feel like he will be able to help you?"

"I really do, Jennifer."

"Good, I'm glad you have faith in him. I think that means a lot if you trust your doctor," added Jennifer.

"Oh, I do trust him!" exclaimed Miranda.

"I just want you back to your normal self."

"Me, too!" exclaimed Miranda. "I know Mardi would like nothing better, but I must say he has been very patient with me."

"I know he has. Mardi is a great guy!"

"I know...I am so blessed to have him. Just think if I

hadn't gone to Prince Edward Island I would never have met him."

"That is so true and I'm sure God had His hand in the matter. He knew you needed a good husband and He sent you there to find him."

"I believe so, too!" Miranda exclaimed with a smile.

Jennifer sure was glad to see her smiling. "Just think what I went through before Gabe and I got together. When I think of how close I came to losing him, it makes me shiver."

"God knew you needed Gabe, so He spared his life so you two could be together. I think you deserve each other."

"I don't know if I deserved him after the way I treated him, but I sure am thankful that things worked out for us. I'm thankful that both of us have wonderful husbands."

"Me, too!"

Chapter 3

The girls went into the house, thinking the guys might be there since it was close to lunch time. They were nowhere in sight. After changing clothes they headed toward the barn. Gabe and Mardi weren't there so Jennifer and Miranda saddled up a couple horses and headed out on the pasture land. They rode about a mile before they spotted their husbands, who were mending some fences. The Jeep was parked nearby.

"Hello Jennifer and Miranda," said Gabe with a big grin. "I see you have returned."

"Yes, we're back," said Jennifer as they dismounted the horses.

Mardi walked over to Miranda and gave her a hug and kiss. "How did the doctor appointment go?" he asked.

"Actually, I think it went well. I was able to talk freely to Dr. Sable and tell him about my nightmares."

"That's great!" exclaimed Mardi. "We just want you to get well!"

"So do I, Mardi."

"When do you go back to see him?"

"In three days. He wants to see me a couple times a week for awhile. Maybe you could go with me next time."

"I will if Gabe doesn't need me here."

"I will arrange to do without you that day, Mardi. You need to go with Miranda."

"Thank you, Gabe. As a boss, you are the BEST!" exclaimed Mardi smiling.

"Thanks, but then you are a great asset to this ranch."

"That's enough guys...you'd better quit before you get the 'big head'," said Jennifer with a laugh.

"There's not much danger of that happening," remarked Gabe.

"He's right," added Mardi.

"Are you guys hungry?" asked Miranda changing the subject.

"Of course we are," they said in unison. "We're always hungry."

"Then let's head to the house. Jennifer and I will fix some lunch for you."

"Sounds good to me," said Mardi.

"Me, too!" exclaimed Gabe.

The girls mounted their horses and headed for home. The guys weren't far behind in the Jeep. Mardi was anxious to hear Gabe's opinion on Miranda. "Don't you think Miranda sounds much better?" he asked as they drove toward the house.

"Yes, I do think she is sounding better and I am so thankful for that!" exclaimed Gabe. "I really hope this doctor can help her."

"Yeah...me, too. I just want my Miranda back!"

"I can understand that," replied Gabe. "I remember what I went through with Jennifer when our son died. Even though it about killed me, I realized I had to be extra strong for her. Even before our marriage, I lost my first wife and unborn baby at the same time. Life has not been easy for me. If it wasn't for the Lord, I never would have made it through all those tragic times."

"You had to be a strong guy, Gabe...to go through all that sadness and survive."

"I couldn't have done it without the Lord," replied Gabe. "He was my strength in time of need. I really think trials make you stronger and strengthen your faith."

"Oh, I agree with you one hundred percent," added Mardi. "I am trusting Him for Miranda's return to good health. I also trust Him to give us the baby we have been wanting for so long."

"Amen to that!"

They arrived at the house and got out of the Jeep and went inside. Miranda and Jennifer were busy in the kitchen. Something sure smelled tantalizing.

Little did they know what was yet to come and how it would change their lives forever...

Chapter 4

Days turned into weeks and weeks into months. Miranda was still seeing Dr. Sable. She seemed to be doing much better and almost back to her old self again. Dr. Sable told her that he felt a couple more trips would end their sessions. He felt that he'd done all he could for her.

Miranda was happy to hear that. Frankly, she was tired of going. Each trip seemed to be the same. She was feeling much better and was ready to get on with her life.

Mardi had been so supportive in her illness and she owed him so much for standing beside her. She wanted to be the best wife ever and hopefully a mother soon. They had been trying for the past few months, but so far... nothing. She really wanted a baby, maybe too much and that could be the reason it wasn't happening. She had even discussed adoption with Mardi, who told her to give it more time. He didn't want to rush into anything. He felt that Miranda would get pregnant one day. Right now, she needed to eat well and gain back her strength. Her body needed to be prepared for the pregnancy.

Mardi knew how much Miranda loved dogs and decided it would be good to have a dog on the ranch. He had gone over to visit their neighbors on the ranch next to them. Robert and Elizabeth Butler were the owners and were in their sixties. Robert was beginning to have health problems and told Mardi that his dog, Maggie, had a litter of puppies which were now one year old. He couldn't bring himself to separate them from their mother but the time had come when he knew he must do something. He asked Mardi if he knew someone who would be willing to take all three dogs. He had already named them Herman, Eddie and Lily. Mardi thought for a minute and told Robert that he would take the dogs to their ranch. Robert was overjoyed because he knew the dogs would have a good home. So Mardi loaded the dogs on his truck, along with the dog houses which Robert gave him and headed for the ranch. He said goodbye to Robert and Elizabeth and headed back to the ranch.

When he arrived home the dogs were all barking. Miranda flew out of the house and ran straight to the truck. "What on earth do you have here?" she asked in surprise and smiling from ear to ear.

"Meet Herman, Eddie and Lily," Mardi replied with pleasure. "They are going to live on the ranch with us."

"Oh, Mardi...I can't believe you did this! Where did you get them?" she asked in suspense. "Who would give away these beautiful dogs?"

"Our neighbors, Robert and Elizabeth Butler. They wanted to find a home for these three dogs. They only kept their mother, Maggie."

"I am so happy to finally have some more dogs. I loved my Siberian Huskies very much, but I know I will love these Labradors just as much. They have such beautiful black shiny coats, too! I can tell they have been well taken care of. Robert and Elizabeth are good people and I know they would only take the best of care of them. Why did they want to get rid of them?"

"He's having health issues. He has Prostate Cancer and is taking radiation treatments. This has zapped his energy and he decided to find a new home for the dogs. Lucky for us that I went over there to see him today."

"That is so true. I think having dogs around will be good for all of us. They have such a way of getting into your heart. They become so close to you, that they seem almost human."

"I know," said Mardi. "I am so glad to see you smiling again!"

"It feels good, too!" she exclaimed. "Tell Robert if he ever wants to find a new home for Maggie, that we'll take her also."

"I'll do that, but I think he will keep her as long as he is able to take care of her."

When Gabe came in from the barn and Jennifer and Isabelle got home that afternoon, they were all surprised to see the new members of the family. Isabelle squealed in delight as she petted all three dogs. They were so excited to see her and acted like they had always known her. From that day forward, she was with the dogs every minute that she was allowed. They watched the back door and waited for her to come outside, at which time they would all come bounding toward her. She wasn't afraid of them even though they were big. They ran and played together while Isabelle squealed if they ganged up on her. Gabe and Jennifer were delighted to see their little daughter so happy. They knew she was lonely since her brother, Isac, had died. The dogs would help fill the void in her life. They were thankful that Robert had given the dogs to Mardi.

As the days and weeks went by they could all see a change in Miranda as well. Bringing the dogs to the ranch was definitely a good thing to do. At last, it seemed that life was about to get back to normal...

Chapter 5

Meanwhile...in the far away city of Manhattan, New York, Caycee Canfield had decided to take some time off from her job and go to Montana to find her relatives. She was a fashion designer with her own clothing line called, 'CAYCEE'.

She knew her mother, Regina, had a twin sister named Rachel, who lived near Billings, Montana. They had never kept in touch due to being separated at birth. Caycee's Mom had died two months ago and this left such an empty feeling in her. She suddenly realized how important family was. That's when she decided to go to Montana and see her Aunt Rachel. She knew Rachel had married a doctor named Parker. That's all she had to go on. She decided to wait until she reached Billings, then she would start the search for her Aunt Rachel.

Caycee landed in Billings around five o'clock on Monday. She had already reserved a room at the Marriott nearby. She would rest awhile and get something to eat and begin her search the next morning. She was up bright and early Tuesday morning and ready to begin her search. She was so excited! Since Rachel married a doctor, she decided the hospitals would be the best place to begin. So she called one after another, to no avail. There was no Dr. Parker working at any of the hospitals. Finally, there was one more place to call, The Billings Medical Hospital

Clinic. By now, she was feeling discouraged and was about to give up.

"Yes, we have a Dr. Parker on staff," said the receptionist in answer to Caycee's question. "Would you like for me to page her?"

"Her?" asked Caycee. "I'm looking for a male doctor by that name."

"I'm sorry; all we have is Dr. Jennifer Parker. I will be glad to page her if you'd like. She may be able to help you."

Caycee thought for a minute and replied, "Yes, please. I would love to talk with her." So she gave her cell phone number to the receptionist and asked her to give it to Dr. Parker.

"Just a moment and I will page her. I'm sure she will get in touch with you soon," responded the receptionist.

"Thank you so much!"

The receptionist immediately paged Dr. Parker. In less than five minutes, Dr. Jennifer Parker returned the hospital's call. "I'm sorry to bother you," said the receptionist. "I just had a call from a girl named Caycee Canfield. She was looking for a male Dr. Parker, which I assume would have been your father. I never told her that your father was deceased. Anyway, she gave me her phone number and wants you to call her."

"Hmmm..." said Jennifer. "That's interesting. Never in my life have I ever heard of Caycee Canfield. I guess I'll give her a call and see what this is all about. Would you please give me her number?"

"Of course," she replied as she gave her the number.

"Thanks for letting me know."

"You're very welcome."

They hung up and Jennifer dialed the number. She

was curious to know what this girl named Caycee wanted with her family.

"Hello," said a pleasant voice on the other end of the line.

"This is Dr. Jennifer Parker. I understand you wanted to talk to me."

"Matter of fact, I did!" exclaimed the voice. "My name is Caycee Canfield and I'm from New York."

"Hello, Caycee. How may I help you?"

"Oh, I guess you are wondering why I want to talk to you. It's really very simple. I think we may be related."

"What?"

"Yes, I was looking for Dr. Parker that married Rachel, who was my mother's twin sister."

"Twin sister?" asked Jennifer in total surprise. "I am Rachel's daughter, but I never heard her speak of a twin sister...not ever! I find that strange! My dad was Mitch Parker and he was a doctor."

"Was???" asked Caycee.

"Oh, yes..." stated Jennifer." He passed away before I was born."

"I am so sorry! How about your mother?"

"She is gone also. She died several years ago due to ovarian cancer."

"Again...I am so sorry!" exclaimed Caycee.

"Thank you," said Jennifer. "What about your mother? What is her name and where does she live?"

"Her name was Regina and she is also deceased. In fact, she passed away a couple months ago with ovarian cancer and that is when I decided to try to find my relatives. She never told me much about her sister. According to her, Rachel never knew they were twins."

"How very sad!" exclaimed Jennifer. "How could she keep that to herself and never let my mom know?"

"It's a long story. If I can meet you somewhere, I will tell you all about it."

"I would love that. I can't help but think of the fact that both of them died with ovarian cancer. That is ironic!"

"When and where can we meet?" asked Caycee.

"I want you to come to the ranch and meet the rest of the family."

"Oh, I would love that," said an excited Caycee.

"My office is next to the hospital. Meet me here at twelve o'clock and I'll take you to the ranch. I can take the afternoon off."

"I'll be there!" exclaimed Caycee excitedly.

They hung up the phone and Jennifer went back to work. She could hardly believe she was about to meet a new cousin that she never knew existed until today. It was all she could do to keep from calling her family, but decided to surprise them. Jennifer was very excited and could hardly wait for twelve o'clock to come. Caycee was on time...Jennifer took one look at her and any doubts she might have had diminished at once. "You have to be Caycee!" exclaimed Jennifer.

"I sure am and you must be Jennifer."

"That I am...I am so happy to meet you Caycee. If I acted strange at first, it was because you have such a resemblance to my sister, Miranda."

"Oh, really? I can't wait to meet her!"

"I can't wait for all the family to meet you! I am so happy that you decided to come to Montana. Otherwise, we would never have known you existed!"

"I tried so hard to get my mother to come here and see her sister, but she wouldn't give in."

"That is such a shame. My mother would have loved it. She was such a family person," said Jennifer. "Well, let's get going. It's a fifteen minute drive to the ranch."

The girls left the office and headed to the parking lot where Jennifer's car was parked. They got into the car and started their journey. Caycee was so excited! The drive was a pleasant one and they reached home at twelve-thirty. They got out of the car and went inside the house. No one was there so the two girls went into the living room to talk. As they were seated, Jennifer spoke up, "I'm glad no one is at home now. It will give us a chance to get acquainted before anyone else arrives. Have you had lunch?"

Caycee smiled at her and exclaimed, "Yes, thank you, I did have an early lunch. I am just so excited!"

"Me, too! I can hardly wait to hear your story! Are you ready to begin?"

"Yes," replied Caycee. Here is how the story goes... "Many years ago Tim Hargrove and his wife, Sandy, had twins girls. Sandy had a very rough delivery and almost died. Going through all this caused her to have a nervous breakdown. She was hospitalized for four months. Meanwhile, her mother took the babies and cared for them while she was in the hospital. After she was released she was never very strong again and was not able to raise both babies. Sandy had a sister, Claire, who was willing to take one of the babies and raise as her own. My mother was the one she took. The family decided to keep this a secret and my mom never knew until she was grown that she had a twin sister. All this time she thought Claire was her mother. Aunt Claire wrestled with the issue for years. She hated to tell her, but knew she deserved to know the truth, no matter how painful it might be. She waited until my mom graduated from high school, then she told her. She was very distressed to hear that her mom had given her up and she had been raised by her aunt, whom she thought was her real mother. She had often wondered why she never looked anything like her two brothers.

Now it was all falling into place... they were her cousins and not her brothers. Aunt Claire decided it was time to tell Regina that she had a twin sister named Rachel. This was even more upsetting to her. She felt cheated that she was the one given away, while her twin got to live with her real mom and dad. She was very bitter for a long time and had no desire to ever meet her sister. Her real mom and dad had been killed in a car accident and her twin sister, Rachel, who was ten at the time, had gone to live with her Aunt Pat Hargrove, who was Tim's sister."

"Wow, this is some story!" exclaimed Jennifer. "It makes me so sad to know these two sisters never met! It seems like they both lost. They missed out on so much by not ever meeting. Even though my mom had her parents for a few years, she was uprooted at the young age of ten. I wonder if the twins were anything alike."

"I brought a picture of my mom," replied Caycee. "Just a minute and I will get it out of my luggage." She proceeded to open her luggage, withdrew the picture and handed it to Jennifer.

Jennifer gasped for breath as she took the picture in her hands. "I can't believe it!!! It's like looking at MY Mother!"

"Really?" asked a stunned Caycee.

"Just a minute and I will show you," said Jennifer as she got up and walked over to the table behind the couch. She picked up her mom's picture and brought it to Caycee.

"I see what you mean!" exclaimed Caycee. "They were definitely identical twins. They look exactly alike. Most people say I look like my mom."

"You do and so does Miranda. It is amazing how much you two resemble."

"You make me even more anxious to meet her!"

"She should be here soon."

"Great!" exclaimed Caycee.

"You know...I can't help but wonder why you never brought your mom out here before she died," stated Jennifer.

"I tried, honest I did," replied Caycee. "She would not come. I don't think she ever got over the fact that she was the one who was given away."

"That is so sad. She must have had a miserable life."

"In a way I think she did," said Caycee sadly. "I worried so much about her and the fact that she never seemed very happy."

"Perhaps things would have been different if she had met her sister. That could have brought closure for her."

"I should have made her come," sighed Caycee. "Now I'm the one feeling guilty."

"You can't feel guilty about something you had no control over. You need to move on and build a new life for yourself. I know you have your Fashions and that is good. Just tell yourself you will not feel guilty anymore."

"Thanks, Jennifer!" exclaimed Caycee. "You've helped me already!" Changing the subject she said, "Tell me about you, Jennifer. Are you married?"

"Yes, I am married to a wonderful man named Gabe Colter. He runs the ranch along with Mardi Carson, who is Miranda's husband. We also have several ranch hands who work here. My brothers aren't interested in the ranch, so it's left up to the sons-in-law to carry on."

"You have brothers, too?"

"Yes, we do. Jordan and Blake Parker are my half brothers from my dad. They are twins who were also separated at birth. Blake was raised by his uncle, Mitch's brother. He didn't know that Mitch was actually his dad until after his dad, Blake Sr. died. I helped him clean out his dad's study and we found young Blake's birth certificate, which had his mother listed. With a little detective work and a DNA test, we found the boys to be twins. This was quite a shock. My dad, Mitch, never knew he was their father. He never knew about me either. He had three children and never knew about any of them."

"Wow! That is so sad! Your family has certainly had its share of troubles!" exclaimed Caycee.

"I know...but I think it has given us a stronger faith in God!

"God? I don't know how I feel about God!" exclaimed Caycee. "I've never been to church, so I don't know much about this religion stuff!"

"I'm so sorry! It seems you were raised much different from us. Did your mother ever go to church?"

"She was made to go when she was a child. When she became older she rebelled and quit going to church. Therefore, I was not raised in church."

"That's so sad! It's never too late to start, you know. Maybe you would like to go with our family while you're here."

"I guess I could do that," she responded.

"Great! I will look forward to taking you with us."

Changing the subject Caycee asked, "Do you have children, Jennifer?"

"Gabe and I have a seven year old daughter, Isabelle. She had a twin brother, Isac, who was killed about a year ago in a riding accident," replied Jennifer with sadness in her eyes.

"Oh, Jennifer, I am so sorry to hear this!" Caycee exclaimed as she got up and gave Jennifer a hug.

"Thank you, Caycee! This past year has been a rough one!"

"I just can't imagine."

"Unless someone goes through it, they can't understand the pain," said Jennifer.

"More about our family... I also have another half brother. His name is Rob Sterling and he is Rachel's son. He and Miranda are full brother and sister. My mom married their dad, Grayson Sterling, several years after Mitch died. You might say we are one big happy family. Of course we still miss our mom and dad very much. Grayson was the only dad I ever knew. He was so good to me and I couldn't have loved him more if he had been my biological dad."

"That certainly is good. So many times step-parents are not good to the children. You sure were lucky," said Caycee.

"It was more than luck, we were blessed."

"Do your brothers live around here?"

"Jordan lives in Billings and does pharmaceutical research. Blake is an actor and lives in Hollywood. Rob is an attorney and lives on Prince Edward Island."

"Prince Edward Island?" asked Caycee. "What's he doing there?"

"He married a girl from there. Her name is Kati Campbell."

"How did he end up there to begin with? How did he meet Kati?" asked Caycee.

"Miranda moved to Prince Edward Island to become partners with Dr. Laura Fisher at Pets Paradise Clinic. She had just completed vet school and moved away. Rob met Kati at Miranda and Mardi's wedding. The met, fell in love, got married and now have a beautiful baby boy named, Robert Grayson Sterling III. They named him after our dad. The rest is history."

"Now I understand," replied Caycee.

About that time the back door opened and in walked

Miranda. She came straight to the living room. She wasn't prepared for the shock she was about to receive. The moment she saw Caycee, she left out a gasp. "Hello," she said looking straight at Caycee. "My name is Miranda."

"Hi Miranda. My name is Caycee Canfield and I am your cousin."

"W-H-A-T?" asked a stunned Miranda. "Where did you come from and how are you related to us?"

"I came from New York and I am your mother's niece."

"How can that be? My mother was an only child."

"No, she wasn't. She had a twin sister named Regina, who was my mother."

Miranda had turned white by this time. She couldn't believe what she was hearing. Could this be true? Why didn't we ever hear about her mom's sister? Why did her mom keep it a secret? She had many unanswered questions. She finally regained her composure and asked, "How did you know about us and how did you find us?"

"If you have time, come sit down and I will tell you the story just as I told your sister."

Miranda walked over and sat on the couch beside Caycee. "First, I have a question for you. Have you noticed how much you and I look alike?"

Laughing Caycee replied, "Of course I have. One would have to be blind to not see it. That should be enough to tell you that I am for real."

"You are right," said Miranda. "It's just such a shock."

"I know...I hope you will understand, once I tell you the story." So, Caycee began telling the story for the second time. Miranda was glued to her every word. An hour later Miranda had more of an understanding about her aunt and cousin. She was sorry that her Aunt Regina had already passed away and she would never meet her. How nice it would have been if the lady had not been stubborn and had come to Montana to meet her twin sister. That would have made her mom, Rachel, so happy.

"Now," said Caycee. "When am I going to meet your daughter?" she asked looking at Jennifer.

"She is upstairs playing. I will go get her. I wanted to have this time alone with you before bringing her downstairs." So, Jennifer went up the steps and told Isabelle that someone wanted to meet her.

"Who is it, Mommy?" she asked.

"Come downstairs and you will see."

Isabelle jumped up from the floor and headed downstairs. She took one look at Caycee and stopped in her tracks. "Who are you?" she asked. "You look like my Aunt Miranda."

Caycee laughed and replied, "I am your mom and Miranda's cousin. That's why I look like Miranda."

"I've never seen you before. Why did you wait so long to come visit us?"

"I just don't know, Isabelle...I just don't know!"

"Well, I'm glad you came," said Isabelle as she turned and ran back up the steps. She was so busy playing and didn't have time for adult conversation.

Chapter 6

The kitchen door opened and in walked Gabe and Mardi. It had been a long, tiring day of work for them. Miranda met them in the kitchen. "Hey, guys...we have company."

"We saw the car with a New York license in the driveway. What VIP came out here for a visit?" asked Gabe.

"You're never going to believe this. We have a new cousin. Her name is Caycee Canfield and her mother was my mother's twin sister!"

"You're kidding, right?" asked Mardi.

"No, I'm not kidding. It's for real!"

"How come we've never heard of her?" asked Gabe.

"It's a long story and we'll have to tell you later. Right now, I want you to come meet Caycee."

Gabe and Mardi followed Miranda into the living room. She was anxious to see their faces once they saw Caycee. She was watching them closely. It was just as she had expected. They both looked like they had seen a ghost. The expression on their faces was priceless. Miranda chuckled to herself.

"Caycee, I'd like for you to meet my husband, Mardi."

Caycee extended her hand, which Mardi accepted. "So nice to meet you, Mardi!" she exclaimed as a 'where have you been all my life' look crossed her face. Miranda was quick to pick up on the look and thought hmmm... this girl needs watching.

"Likewise," said Mardi as sincere as he could be. He never noticed anything out of the ordinary. "Although, I must admit this was quite a shock," he added.

"The fact that I'm here or that I look so much like Miranda?" she asked with a chuckle.

"Both, I guess. Anyway, welcome to Montana."

"Thank you, Mardi. Now, who's this other good looking guy?" asked Caycee.

"Caycee, I'd like for you to meet my husband, Gabe," replied Jennifer.

They shook hands and Gabe welcomed her to the ranch. Looking him straight in the eye Caycee said, "It seems that all the handsome ones are already taken. That's just my luck."

"I'm sure you meet plenty of men," said Jennifer.

"Oh, I do, but so far none of them has put a ring on my finger."

"By the way guys, Caycee, is a fashion designer with her own clothing line."

"That is very exciting!" exclaimed Miranda. "You hadn't told me that!"

"There was time for that later. We had family business to discuss first," she said with a smile crossing her beautiful face.

"Ladies, if you'll excuse us, we'll be back down after we take a shower," said Gabe as he and Mardi left to go upstairs.

"We'll take you out to eat since we don't have any dinner cooked," said Jennifer to Caycee. "Follow me and I will show you to your room. You might want to freshen up a bit. We'll leave as soon as the guys are ready."

"Thank you for your hospitality," said Caycee to Jennifer. "Actually, I am quite hungry. I haven't eaten since ten-thirty this morning."

"You should have told me and I would have found you something to tide you over."

"I was so excited that I forgot that I hadn't eaten. I didn't realize I was hungry until now."

Thirty minutes later the guys were dressed and came downstairs. Both were dressed in jeans and a knit shirt. Caycee was staring at them as they descended the stairs. Jennifer and Miranda both noticed it. Miranda knew she and Jennifer needed to have a talk and soon.

"You guys look ravishing!" exclaimed Caycee with a big smile.

"Thanks," they responded in unison as a big grin crossed their faces. This never went unnoticed by their wives either.

"Jennifer, may I speak to you for a minute?" asked Miranda. "In private?"

"Sure," replied Jennifer as they walked into the kitchen. "What's up?"

"What's up...is Caycee! Surely you have noticed how she is coming on to our husbands!"

"I wouldn't say she is 'coming on' but she is definitely interested in them, I think."

"I am going to have a talk with Mardi. He needs to know where to draw the line. Guys don't always see when a woman is coming on to them. We are so much more aware of these things," added Miranda.

"I will talk to Gabe, too!" exclaimed Jennifer. "I know he would never do anything to hurt me but it won't hurt to warn him about Caycee."

"You are so right. I am wondering if she might try to use her looks to entice Mardi. With her looking so much like me, it might be easy for him to fall prey to her charm."

"You know...I hadn't thought of that. We will both keep an eye on her," replied Jennifer.

"It was nice to meet her but I find myself wishing she hadn't come to Montana. We never knew about her anyway and life would have gone on without ever knowing her."

"That's true," replied Jennifer. "Maybe she will soon become bored on the ranch and want to go back to the big city."

"We can only hope. I guess we had better get back in the living room before she devours both our husbands," laughed Miranda.

As they entered the living room they didn't like what they saw. Caycee was standing close to Mardi and looking up into his face as she talked to him. She had an innocent looking smile on her face. The guys might buy it, but not Miranda. Caycee was after her man and Mardi was allowing it without even realizing what was happening.

Chapter 7

"Are you guys ready to go?" asked Miranda looking straight at Mardi and Caycee without a smile.

"We're ready," responded Mardi. "Where are we going to eat?"

"Jennifer can choose a place since she works in Billings. I'm sure she knows more about the restaurants than the rest of us do."

"What do you guys feel like eating tonight?" asked Jennifer.

"You choose," replied Gabe.

"How about we go to REX...SEAFOOD, STEAK HOUSE? That is my favorite place to eat."

"Sounds good to me," replied Gabe.

"Me, too!" exclaimed Mardi.

"Sounds like a good place to go," added Caycee.

Jennifer took Isabelle by the hand and led her to the car. They all got in and headed to Billings. Gabe drove and Jennifer insisted Mardi ride in front. The girls all rode in the second seat of the van, except for Isabelle, who rode in her car seat on the third seat.

They arrived at the restaurant about twenty minutes later. Gabe and Mardi had talked the whole time, with Caycee interrupting every chance she got. Jennifer and Miranda didn't have much to say. They were both getting their fill of Caycee. Both were hoping she would make her stay at the ranch a short one. Caycee had other ideas...she was in no hurry to leave the ranch.

"I am so enjoying my visit with my new family," Caycee stated as she got out of the van. "You have made me feel so welcome. I might just stay for a couple months."

Miranda and Jennifer exchanged glances. "You are family so we are happy to have you," responded Jennifer trying to sound sincere.

"Thanks, Jennifer. How about you Miranda?" she asked.

"Oh, sure," replied Miranda trying to smile. Inside, she had a different feeling. She was feeling threatened by this woman. They might look alike, but inside they were totally different. Miranda was not the scheming woman that Caycee was. She could see right through her.

"Well," piped Caycee. "I think I've found my second home."

By now they were inside the restaurant and neither Jennifer nor Miranda responded to her last statement. They hated to be rude, but more and more they were learning that she was nothing like them. She had a wild streak in her and it was beginning to show. If she stayed for a couple months, they wondered what all she would try during that time. Both of them knew she needed to be watched, as far as their husbands were concerned. Gabe and Mardi were naïve when it came to women like Caycee. She was of the world and they weren't prepared to deal with the likes of her.

Somehow they got through dinner and everyone tried to act normal, except for Caycee. Then she probably was acting normal...for her. It would take some time for her cousins to get used to her. All through dinner she made sure she was the center of attention. Jennifer and Miranda just sat back and observed. Caycee made sure that she held the attention of Gabe and Mardi. "Guys," she spoke up. "I want you to teach me to ride a horse."

Caught off guard, Gabe and Mardi looked at each other with question. "Well," replied Gabe. "I think someone on the ranch can teach you."

"NO, I don't want just SOMEONE...I want one of you guys!" she exclaimed.

Jennifer and Miranda were watching their husbands squirm and wondered what words would come out of their mouth next.

"I don't know," said Gabe. "I stay really busy. I don't think I have time for riding lessons. Sorry! I'll talk to the other cowhands and maybe we can spare one of them."

"I told you I don't want one of them!" she exclaimed in a louder tone. "How about you, Mardi? Can you spare a few minutes each day for me?"

Mardi glanced at Miranda, hoping she would come to his rescue. Miranda never said a word. She just sat there, waiting to see how Mardi would respond to Caycee.

"Well, I don't know..." replied Mardi.

"What's wrong with you guys? Are you afraid of me?" she asked short tempered.

"Oh no, that's not it. We are just very busy on the ranch," replied Mardi.

"Then I will pay you to give me riding lessons," she spoke up.

"That won't be necessary," said Gabe. "If Mardi wants to give you thirty minutes a day, I can spare him."

"Great!" exclaimed Caycee smiling. "Thank you!"

Mardi gave Gabe a look that was not a good one. If looks could kill, Gabe would have dropped dead at that moment. "Are you sure you can spare me, Gabe?" he asked.

"Yes, Mardi. We are doing this for family," he explained.

"One week of lessons and that is it!" exclaimed Mardi as he looked straight at Caycee.

"Okay," she replied. "I will take what I can get."

Miranda felt relieved to hear that Mardi promised Caycee only one week. She could deal with that. Surely there wasn't too much that Caycee could do in a week...

They continued their dinner without any more 'horse' talk. From then on the conversation was minimal. Jennifer and Miranda had little to say. If Gabe and Mardi noticed, they never let on. What could have been a pleasant evening for the sisters was ruined by their cousin.

After the meal was finished, Jennifer suggested it was time to go home. The bill was paid and a generous tip left for their waitress. They left the restaurant and headed for the van. Seating arrangement was as before. The trip home had very little conversation. It seemed that everyone was "talked out." Jennifer and Miranda were in deep thought...

They arrived back at the ranch and everyone turned in. It had been a long day. The sisters wondered how many more long days were ahead of them. This was Caycee's first day on the ranch and already Miranda and Jennifer were having a problem dealing with her. What could have been a joyous reunion was turning into a nightmare. Neither of them liked the way she was coming on to their husbands. Maybe Caycee thought they were dumb...but it was so obvious to both of them what she was trying to do. They would watch her closely...

Up early the next morning, Caycee was already in the kitchen with the guys when Miranda walked into the kitchen. "Good morning, Miranda!" exclaimed Caycee with a beaming smile.

"Morning," replied Miranda. "You're up early and in a good mood."

"Oh, yes, it's a beautiful morning!" she exclaimed. "I wanted to get up early so Mardi could start my riding lessons today."

"Oh, so soon?" asked Miranda reluctantly.

"There's no time like the present," chirped Caycee with a smile.

"I guess," stated Miranda as she poured herself a cup of coffee. She looked at Mardi to see what kind of expression was on his face. He didn't look too happy. He had gotten caught up in Caycee's scheme and there wasn't much he could do about it without being rude.

"So, my friend," said Caycee looking at Mardi. "What time do you want to start my riding lesson?"

"How about eight o'clock?" asked Mardi with no expression. "I have some other things I need to do first."

"Eight o'clock is fine," replied Caycee with a smile.

"Be out at the stable then. Don't be late! I have work to do, you know."

"I'll be there. I am very excited!" she answered him excitedly.

Miranda picked up on the excitement in her voice. She was thinking to herself, "I just bet you are!"

The guys left for the stable and Caycee went back to her room. Thirty minutes later she reappeared. She was dressed in super tight jeans and a scantily cut knit shirt that showed her well endowed bust line. Miranda took all of this in. It appeared to her that Caycee was trying to look as sexy as she could for Mardi. This did not sit well with Miranda. She knew what Caycee was trying to do. She had seen her kind before.

A few minutes before eight, Caycee left the house without saying another word to Miranda. Jennifer appeared in the kitchen a few minutes after Caycee left. She was dressed ready for work. "Sit down and have a cup of coffee, Jennifer," said Miranda. "There is something I want to tell you."

"What is it, little sister?" asked Jennifer as she poured herself a cup of coffee. She came over to the table and sat down.

Miranda poured herself another cup and sat back down. "It's Caycee!" exclaimed Miranda. "I don't know how much more of her I can take!"

"What's she done now?" asked Jennifer earnestly.

"You should have seen how she is dressed for her 'ride' with MY husband!"

"Oh, really?"

"Oh, really!" exclaimed Miranda. "She is wearing skin tight jeans and a skimpy little top that leaves nothing to the imagination! I know what she is trying to do!"

"Wow! I'm sorry Miranda!"

"Me, too...That girl is after my husband!"

"You need to have a talk with Mardi tonight. Chances are he doesn't even realize what she is trying to do."

"I know...men can be so gullible. I plan to have a serious talk with him tonight."

"Good! You go girl!" exclaimed Jennifer. "Now, I have to leave for work. I don't want to be late. Have a good day, Miranda and try not to worry. Everything will be okay. Mardi loves you very much!"

"I know he does. See you tonight. Have a good day."

"Thanks and bye Miranda."

"Bye, Jennifer."

Miranda got up, walked to the sink and started washing the dirty dishes. Her mind was not on her task. All she could think of was Mardi and Caycee out riding together.

Meanwhile, out in the stable Mardi and Caycee were preparing to start her riding lessons. He was teaching her how to saddle the horse and how to mount. She pretended to need help mounting, so Mardi gave her a boost. They started in a slow walk. He wanted her to get the feel of the horse for awhile. Later they increased their speed to a trot. Caycee was excited. What Mardi didn't know was that Caycee was already an excellent rider. She would make sure he never knew. She pretended to be so helpless, so he would be very attentive to her. She knew how to work men. She'd had plenty of practice.

They rode side by side for half an hour. Caycee was enjoying this immensely. Mardi didn't suspect a thing. She chuckled to herself. Men are so dumb, she thought. They arrived back at the stable and Mardi showed her how to groom her horse. All the while she was acting so helpless. She had a grin on her face as she walked back to the house.

Miranda just happened to be looking out the window as Caycee was approaching. The grin on her face did not escape Miranda. "Did you have a good lesson?" she asked as Caycee entered the house.

"Matter of fact, I did. Mardi is a great teacher!" she exclaimed. "I can't wait until tomorrow. We had a great time together!"

This was about more than Miranda could take. She turned and walked out of the room. She knew if she stayed, she would say something she might regret. Caycee sure was getting under her skin! She didn't seem the least bit concerned how she was coming on to another woman's husband. This made Miranda's temperature rise. She rarely ever got mad but this was another story. She would fight for her man!

Cacyee stayed in her room most of the day and that

made Miranda happy. She didn't even want to see her. She had only been here two days and she was about to turn Miranda's world upside down.

When Mardi came in for dinner later that day, Miranda just had to inquire about Caycee's riding lesson that morning. "How did Caycee do on her first riding lesson?"

"She did fair," replied Mardi. "In fact, she was slower learning than I thought she would be. It may take more than a week to teach her."

This made Miranda's blood boil. "You only promised her one week!" she exclaimed.

"I know, but I think it will take longer."

"Can't you see what she is doing?" asked Miranda with a raised voice.

"What are you talking about?" he asked with raised eyebrows.

"She is after you, Mardi and that is plain and simple!"

Mardi laughed, "That is crazy, Miranda!"

"Maybe it is, but it is true! If you weren't so blind you could see through her!"

"I think you are misjudging her, Miranda."

"I don't think so...even Jennifer can see it."

"She has only been here two days. I think you should be nicer to her," expressed Mardi.

"Sounds like she already has YOU under her spell!"

"No, she doesn't. I can take care of myself," he added.

"Make sure you do!" exclaimed Miranda as she walked out of the room. She intended to discuss this with Jennifer and get her feelings on the situation.

Chapter 8

Miranda had dinner ready when Jennifer arrived home from work. Caycee was still in her room. Doing what? Miranda had no idea and really didn't care, as long as she stayed out of her sight. She didn't like the feeling that had crept over her the past two days, but it was not her fault. Caycee had rubbed her the wrong way when she started flirting with her husband.

The dinner was on the table and the men had come in from work and were getting their hands washed. Caycee hadn't come down yet. "Jennifer, will you go tell Caycee to come to dinner?" asked Miranda.

"Sure," replied Jennifer as she headed toward the stairs.

Shortly both girls entered the dining room and sat down at the table. Isabelle was already seated. Gabe and Mardi soon joined them. Miranda was the last to sit down. The blessing was said and they began passing the food around. Miranda noticed that Caycee never ate much. Was she mad or trying to keep her slim figure?

"So, how was your day, Caycee?" asked Jennifer trying to draw her into the conversation.

"It was okay," she replied looking down at her plate.

"Are you all right?" asked Jennifer with concern.

"I'm okay," she said still looking at her plate. She wasn't very convincing.

"Is there something I can do for you, Caycee?" asked Jennifer.

"No, thank you," she answered without looking up.

Jennifer knew something was wrong. She decided another approach might work. "Caycee, did you bring a portfolio of your fashion clothes with you?"

Caycee looked up for the first time and smiled, "Matter of fact, I did."

"I would love to see it," responded Jennifer.

"Sure thing," added Caycee. "It's still in my luggage, so I will go upstairs and get it. I'll be back down shortly."

"Great," said Jennifer.

While she was gone upstairs Jennifer asked Mardi how the riding lesson went. "It was a little slow," he replied. "I think it may take more than a week for her to really learn."

Jennifer looked at Miranda, who had an unhappy look on her face. She knew this was causing trouble between her and Mardi. She could see that Miranda felt threatened by Caycee's presence in the house. What could they do about it? It would be rude to ask her to leave. She needed to think and perhaps devise a plan.

Caycee returned with her portfolio and laid it on the table. Jennifer and Miranda had cleared a spot for her. Caycee opened it and started showing them her designs.

Jennifer and Miranda were breathless. She was very good! They were surprised at just how good she was. As she turned the pages, each one seemed more beautiful than the previous one. Even little Isabelle was in awe.

"Your dresses are so pretty, Caycee," piped Isabelle.

"Why, thank you, Isabelle!" exclaimed Caycee with a smile. "I can see you have a flair for fashion."

"You think so?" asked Isabelle.

"Most definitely, little one."

Isabelle thought a minute and replied, "Maybe I will be a fashion designer when I grow up. I would like to be just like you!"

"That's an excellent idea, young Isabelle!" exclaimed Caycee. "I bet you would be great!"

"Let me give you some paper and colored pencils and see what you can draw."

"Yeah!!!" shouted Isabelle as she reached for the paper and pencils. She immediately started drawing a dress by looking at Caycee's sketch. She did well considering she was only seven years old. After she finished, she showed her drawing to everyone waiting for their approval.

"That's excellent!" exclaimed her mother.

"You have an eye for fashion," added her dad.

"What do you think, Aunt Miranda?" asked Isabelle.

"Oh, I think you're very good!"

"What do you think, Uncle Mardi?" she asked.

"You're going to be the best fashion designer ever," he replied with a laugh.

"Better than Caycee?" she asked.

"I never said that, but I think you will be equally as good."

"I know you can do it, Isabelle!" exclaimed Caycee.

"Well, I guess I know what I will do when I grow up!" she exclaimed. Looking at Caycee, she asked, "Will I have to go to college?"

"Of course, my dear," answered Caycee. "There are lots of things you will learn in fashion school that you would never know otherwise."

"Okay," she said. "I will go to college."

"That's enough for tonight, Isabelle," said her Mother. "It's time for bed. Give the pencils and pad back to Caycee."

"Oh, no...she can keep them. I have more. How can she learn to draw if she doesn't have the right equipment?" asked Caycee.

"What do you say, Isabelle?" asked Jennifer.

"Thank you, Caycee!" she exclaimed as she gave her a big hug.

Chapter 9

How quickly things fall into place. Little did Jennifer know that Caycee would expose her scheme so soon. The following Saturday at lunch, Caycee announced that she was ready to take the horse out by herself. Mardi was apprehensive about her riding alone so soon, but never said anything. He knew how Miranda felt about him spending time with Caycee, so he kept his mouth shut to avoid trouble.

Jennifer had a plan! Caycee excused herself from the table and went to her room to change into her riding clothes. Jennifer pulled Miranda aside where the men couldn't hear and told her of her plan.

"I like that idea," said Miranda with a big grin on her face.

So the girls got changed and left the house a few minutes after Caycee. They gave her time to saddle her horse and leave. They hurried and were not far behind her. They knew the land and knew how to keep out of sight.

"LOOK AT HER!" exclaimed Jennifer. "She is no beginner."

"I agree," said Miranda. "She had us all fooled, but not anymore! I can't wait to tell Mardi."

Caycee was riding like the wind. She sat tall in the saddle and rode like a professional. You could tell she'd had plenty of experience on a horse. This made Miranda even more angry at her. Now she knew for certain that Caycee was after her husband.

"Can you believe her?" asked Miranda angrily.

"I must say, I am surprised she would stoop this low. Why would she want to take your husband? I'm sure she has plenty of suitors."

"I don't know, but she is in for the fight of her life if she doesn't drop it."

"Maybe I should have a talk with her," suggested Jennifer.

"Don't say anything to her yet. Let's see how far she will go."

"As you wish, Miranda."

The girls turned their horses and headed back to the stable. As luck would have it, Mardi happened to be there. "Do we ever have something to tell you, Mardi!" exclaimed Miranda.

"What is all this excitement about?" asked Mardi.

"Caycee is a fraud!" exclaimed Miranda.

"What do you mean?" asked Mardi in surprise.

"She let you think she couldn't ride just so you would give her lessons. She can ride like the wind. Jennifer and I just saw her."

Mardi was speechless and looked at Jennifer. "It's true, Mardi," said Jennifer.

"You've got to be kidding me!" he exclaimed.

"I wish we were," replied Miranda. "Caycee is after you hot and heavy!"

"I don't think so," replied Mardi.

"Then you're blind!" shouted Miranda angrily. "Jennifer and I can see right through her. I guess maybe that's because we are women."

"Maybe so..." he added with a worried look on his

face. "Miranda, you know I would never do anything to hurt you."

"I know that," replied Miranda. "I trust you; it's Caycee that I don't trust!"

"I'll just try to stay away from her and the riding lessons are over!" he exclaimed.

"Good," replied Miranda. "That's a relief to know."

Mardi left and the girls groomed their horses. They were just finishing when Caycee arrived back at the stable. "Did you have a good ride?" asked Miranda.

"Matter of fact, I did. I am really learning to ride."

"Cut the crap!" exclaimed Miranda with a raised voice. "Jennifer and I both saw you riding like the wind. We're not dumb enough to believe you are a beginner."

Caycee laughed and explained, "Mardi is a good teacher and I'm a fast learner."

"Do you really expect us to believe that? How dumb do you think we are?" asked Miranda angrily.

"Apparently not dumb enough," laughed Caycee as she tossed her long golden hair behind her shoulders.

"Now that you are busted, I think we need to talk," suggested Jennifer looking straight at Caycee.

"About what?" she asked so nonchalantly.

"I think you know about WHAT! Don't play dumb with me, cousin! I'm on to you!" exclaimed Jennifer.

"I haven't done anything wrong," said Caycee.

"Maybe not, but we are going to nip this in the bud before anything does happen."

"What are you talking about?" asked Caycee so innocently.

"You know very well that you are coming on to Mardi. He may not see it, but Miranda and I surely do. We won't stand for it. Either you shape up or you're out of here!"

"That's not a very nice way to treat your cousin!" exclaimed Caycee.

"You haven't acted very nice since you arrived either. GET YOUR OWN MAN!" exclaimed Miranda. "You are NOT getting mine!"

"Simmer down, my naïve little cousin," spoke Caycee to Miranda. "If your man wants me, there is nothing you can do about it!"

"We'll see about that!" shouted Miranda with fire in her eyes.

"Oh, I think Mardi loves you, but I think he is falling for me, too. We look so much alike, maybe he will have a hard time choosing between us," Caycee suggested with a laugh.

Miranda was really angry after this statement. "In your dreams!" shouted Miranda. "Mardi would never be unfaithful to me!"

"How can you be so sure?" asked Caycee. "If the situation is right, you don't know what he might do!"

"I happen to know Mardi. We love each other very much and he would never do anything to risk destroying our marriage," replied Miranda with much confidence.

"We'll see about that!" exclaimed Caycee.

"Caycee, I am giving you a choice. Either you straighten up and quit flirting with Mardi, or I want you to leave," spoke Jennifer.

"I'll be leaving soon anyway," she replied with a nonchalant attitude.

"I think that would be for the best!" exclaimed Jennifer. "I am not going to stand by and watch you destroy my sister and her marriage!"

"Are you your sister's keeper?" she asked with a smirk.

"Let's just say that I will do anything and everything

I have to do to protect her. The same goes for all my family."

"Well, aren't you something? The almighty Dr. Parker!"

"I am proud of who I am," stated Jennifer. "Can you say the same?"

"Of course, I can! I am a big fashion designer!" exclaimed Caycee with a complacent grin.

"That you are," replied Jennifer. "Why don't you start acting like an adult instead of a child?"

"Just who do you think you are to tell me how to act?" she asked angrily.

Jennifer started walking away, "This conversation is over!" she exclaimed. "As I said before, shape up or ship out!"

"Yes, ma'am," stated Caycee and left the stable, heading to the house.

Jennifer and Miranda soon followed and Caycee was nowhere to be seen. They assumed she was in her room. Later, after the sisters had cooked dinner, Jennifer went to the bottom of the stairs and gave a yell to Caycee. "Dinner's ready, Caycee!" There was no answer... Jennifer called the second time and still no answer. Mumbling to herself Jennifer said, "You can just starve for all I care."

As she was entering the kitchen, the phone rang. "I'll get it," stated Jennifer.

"Good," replied Miranda. "I'm busy."

"Hello, Parker ranch. This is Jennifer speaking."

"JENNIFER!!!" exclaimed an excited male voice on the other end of the line. "It's Harley...Harley Brock from the beach in California."

"HARLEY!!!" shouted Jennifer. "How in the world are you? I never expected to hear from you again!"

"I was just thinking about you and did a little research

until I found you. Thank God for the miracle of computers! So...how have you been and what are you doing?"

"I'm doing great. I have a wonderful husband and a beautiful daughter. I have been living on the ranch for several years....actually ever since I graduated from medical school. I realized this is where I belong. I work at Billings Clinic Hospital. My office is adjacent to the hospital.

"I'm glad things are going well for you, Jennifer. How are your parents?" asked Harley.

"They are both gone," replied Jennifer in a softer tone. Harley could hear the change in her voice.

"I am so sorry! What happened to them?" he asked.

Mom died with ovarian cancer when I was in the beginning of medical school. Dad died in his sleep, from a heart attack. He blamed himself for Isac's death and he never got over it."

"Who is Isac?" asked Harley with the most sincerity.

"Isac was our son. He was Isabelle's twin."

"Oh, Jennifer, I didn't know. I am so sorry!" he exclaimed.

"What happened?" he asked.

"There was a riding accident. Isac was riding his pony and it threw him. He died a few days later."

"You said your dad blamed himself."

"Yes, he did. He had bought each of the twins their own pony and that particular day, Dad and Isac were riding together. Suddenly, without warning, Isac took off riding like the wind. There was no stopping him. Dad tried but Isac kept going. Dad was riding after him and got there just as the pony threw him. Dad blamed himself for the accident."

"It doesn't sound like it was his fault," replied Harley.

"That's what we all tried to tell him but he never got over it."

"Oh, that's a shame," stated Harley. "How's the rest of your family?"

"They're doing well. Miranda and her husband, Mardi, also live on the ranch. Mardi and my husband, Gabe, run the ranch. Of course they have plenty of help from the hired hands."

"That's great! I'm sure you love having your sister with you. How about your brothers?" he asked.

"Rob is a lawyer and is living on Prince Edward Island. He is married and has a little boy. Jordan is in Pharmacology research and lives in Billings. He is also married and has a little girl.

I also have another brother, Blake, who is an actor in Hollywood. He's still single and looking. He and Jordan are twins, but that is a long story."

"Wow!" he exclaimed. "What made Rob decide to move to Prince Edward Island?" asked Harley. "I guess I'm just curious."

Jennifer laughed, "Well, it all started with Miranda. She is a Veterinarian and moved to Prince Edward Island to become a partner at Pets Paradise Clinic in Charlottetown. We all went to her wedding and that is where Rob met his future bride, Miss Katie Campbell."

"How exciting!" exclaimed Harley. "It sounds like your family is doing well."

"Actually, we are," said Jennifer. "Now that's enough about me...tell me about you!"

"How would you like to see me?" asked Harley with a chuckle.

"I would LOVE to see you, Harley!" exclaimed Jennifer. "Why don't you come to the ranch for a visit?"

"That's exactly what I was thinking about," he replied with a laugh.

"Oh, really?" asked Jennifer with delight. "We would love to have you! When can you come?"

"How about in two weeks?"

"Two weeks would be fine," she responded. "I can't wait to tell my family!"

"Are you sure it will be okay with them?"

"Of course it will. We love having company. In fact, we have company now. Actually she is a relative and it's a long story."

"Okay, Jennifer...I will look forward to seeing you and meeting your family."

"Sounds great!" Give me a call as soon as you get into Billings and I will pick you up at the airport. Here's my cell phone number." She gave him her number and they said their goodbyes and hung up.

Jennifer walked back into the kitchen with an excited look on her face. "You're never going to believe who just called!"

"It must have been important to keep you away from the dinner table," said Miranda. "We got tired waiting on you and decided to go ahead and eat."

"That's fine with me," replied Jennifer glancing around the table. "Where's Caycee?"

"She said she wasn't hungry. I guess she's still in her room," replied Miranda.

"She'll get over it," stated Jennifer. "Anyway...I just have to tell you... My friend, Harley Brock, whom I met in California over ten years ago, is who I was talking to."

"What? Who's he?" asked Gabe. "I haven't heard of him."

"I met him at the beach when my parents first took me to California. That was before I started medical school. It seems forever ago! No, Gabe, we never actually dated.

We were just friends. Anyway…he is coming to the ranch for a visit in two weeks."

"He is?" asked a surprised Miranda.

"Yes, he is. It will be good to see him again. I know all of you will like him."

"Where does he live and what kind of work does he do?" asked Gabe.

"The last I knew he went to New York to become a magazine editor. I don't know if he's with the same company, but we'll soon find out."

"Wonder why he is coming west?" asked Gabe.

"He never said," replied Jennifer. "I was so surprised to find out he was coming though. I never thought I would ever see him again. We hung out at the beach and surfed a few days. Then he came to my apartment to tell me that he was leaving California. Matter of fact, Gabe, he was there when you called me. He told me to go to you. He could tell that you were the love of my life."

"Sounds like a wise man to me," laughed Gabe as he leaned over and gave Jennifer a kiss. "I am anxious to meet this man."

"You will like him, Gabe, I promise!"

"I have an idea," laughed Miranda. While he's here visiting us, just maybe we can connect him with Caycee."

"I wouldn't wish that on him," responded Jennifer. "He's much too nice for her."

"Don't you think you're being a bit too harsh?" asked Gabe.

"Not on your life," answered Jennifer. "Besides, he may be married. We never got that far in our conversation. So, Miranda…forget about that idea."

"O-k-a- y…If he's as nice as you say, I wouldn't want her to have him."

Chapter 10

The next morning Caycee came down for breakfast. She acted like nothing had happened. "Are you hungry?" asked Miranda as she was setting the food on the table.

"I'm starving!" she exclaimed as she sat down. The others joined her and they had a pleasant breakfast. No one mentioned Harley Brock. Conversation was general talk. Caycee was quieter than usual and concentrated on her food. Everyone was thankful that she was quiet.

After breakfast the men left for the barn. Jennifer had to get ready for work, so that left Miranda and Caycee alone, except for Isabelle.

"Hello, little one," said Caycee to Isabelle. "What are you doing today?"

"I have to go to school," she replied with a sigh.

"Don't you like going to school?"

"Sometimes...but sometimes I would rather stay home with Aunt Miranda," she replied.

"You have to go to school to learn, my little friend. If you are going to be a fashion designer like me, it will take many years of schooling."

"I know..." she sighed as she left the kitchen and went upstairs to get ready for school.

"Well, that leaves you and me together, doesn't it?"

"I guess it does," replied Miranda.

"Do you think we can be civil to each other today?" asked Caycee with a grin.

"I certainly hope so," answered Miranda. "I don't like to argue."

"So what are your plans for today?"

"The same as usual, I guess," replied Miranda.

"I've been thinking...I need to go shopping. Since I don't have a car, would you mind driving me in? We might even learn to enjoy each other's company. We could have lunch together."

"I could do that. In fact, there are some things I need to pick up as well."

"What time do you want to leave?" asked Caycee.

"How about ten o'clock?"

"Sounds fine to me... and Miranda...THANK YOU!"

"You're welcome."

Caycee left and went upstairs to take a shower and get ready. Miranda cleaned up the kitchen, and then went upstairs to get ready. Shortly before ten, they were ready to go. They both got into Miranda's car and headed toward Billings. Shopping was better there than in Laurel. To Miranda's surprise, they actually had a good time talking on the way. This is how it should be, thought Miranda. She was careful to keep the conversation light and not mention Mardi's name. She felt this was best.

"So...," said Miranda trying to be polite and interested. "Where is your next job taking you?"

"Oh, I never told you and Jennifer...but I am going to Paris in two months. I will have a big showing there with lots of celebrities in attendance."

"That is GREAT!" exclaimed Miranda. "I know you must be excited!"

"Most definitely, I am!" Caycee exclaimed with a grin.

"I have dreamed of this day! I have worked very hard trying to make it happen!"

"I am so proud of you, Caycee!" exclaimed Miranda with a big, sincere smile.

"Thank you, Miranda. That means a lot coming from you. We may have gotten off on the wrong foot, but I hope all that is behind us. After all, we are cousins!"

"I know...I'm sorry for being hateful with you."

"That's okay," replied Caycee. "I asked for it. I shouldn't have flirted with your husband. I was just having fun."

"The fun was at my expense though," said Miranda.

"I know and I am very sorry," said Caycee. "I promise to behave myself the remainder of my time here."

"That sounds good and you are welcome to stay as long as you behave."

The girls arrived at the Billings Mall and parked the car. They were excited to be going shopping and decided to make a day of it. Caycee was looking for some new lingerie to take on her trip to Paris. Since she wore her own fashions, she didn't need to look for anything in the clothing line.

They shopped at Victoria's Secret and Caycee found several things she liked. When they left the store she was carrying two bags full of lingerie. Miranda had decided to buy something new to spice up her marriage. She bought a couple teddies that should do the job. One was red with lace and ruffles and the other was black with beads and lace. She couldn't wait to see Mardi's eyes light up, as she knew they would. She realized that she needed to do more to make him feel wanted and keep their marriage alive. Since her dad died things had somewhat changed between them. She never felt like making love anymore and she thought it must be due to her depression. The psychiatrist had helped her but she needed to start helping herself some too! After seeing the way Caycee had flirted with Mardi, it was enough to convince her that she needed to be more attentive to him. She didn't think he would cheat on her but in the back of her mind she couldn't be sure. After all he was a man and if things weren't going well at home, sometimes they do stray. She was bound and determined not to let that happen. She knew she had a challenge ahead of her.

The girls shopped all day. They had to make several trips to the car and unload their merchandise. They were having a wonderful time! Caycee is fun, thought Miranda. I'm glad I decided to give her a second chance.

They had lunch in the food court and acted like teenagers as they ate and enjoyed each other's company. Anyone observing them would have thought they were best friends. They laughed and talked for over an hour. They talked about a little of everything. When they left the mall, each girl felt she had a better understanding of the other. Miranda was glad they had this opportunity to get together with no one else around. They needed this time alone...

The ride home was even better than the one going to the mall. They had discovered a lot about each other. Miranda never thought she would admit it, but she was actually glad that Caycee had come for a visit. She knew Jennifer would want to know all about their shopping trip and also knew that she would be surprised that they had so much fun. She couldn't wait to tell her. Maybe one Saturday the three of them could go shopping together.

They pulled into the driveway and got out of the car. Jennifer met them at the door. "It's about time you two were getting here," she said smiling.

"We got here in time to cook dinner, Jennifer," said Miranda. "Were you worried?"

"Of course I was," replied Jennifer with a laugh. "I was afraid I was going to have to cook and you know you're a much better cook than I am."

Miranda had to laugh. "Well, I do know that my dear sister, but you need to practice some, or you will forget how to cook."

"Fat chance of that happening," replied Jennifer. "Anyway, how was your day?"

"We had a great time," said Miranda.

"Really?" asked Jennifer in surprise. "Did you buy a lot of pretty things?"

"Of course we did," responded Caycee. "Victoria's Secret was happy to see us coming."

"Oh really?" asked Jennifer. "After dinner I want to see what all you bought."

"That will be fun," replied Caycee. "I'll be glad to show you what I bought to take to Paris."

"To Paris?" asked Jennifer in surprise.

"Yes, to Paris. I guess I forgot to mention it to you. In all the excitement of coming to the ranch, the fashion world has taken a second place."

"That is your means of living though," stated Jennifer. "You can't forget that."

"Oh, I haven't forgotten...I'm taking a break," she explained with a laugh.

"We're glad you came," said Miranda. Then she turned and looked at her sister, who had a curious look on her face.

Jennifer needed to have a talk with Miranda and find out what was going on. Miranda had returned from the mall with a different attitude about Caycee. What had happened? She had no idea, but was determined to find out. "What else did you do at the mall?" she asked.

"Oh, we went to a lot of stores. We actually did more

looking than anything. I have something funny to tell you...Miranda and I were mistaken for twins by several different people."

"Really?" asked Jennifer. "I can see how that could happen."

"It was a lot of fun. When we told people we weren't twins, but first cousins, the look on their faces was priceless. Actually I think they thought we were lying."

"Did you laugh when you told them?" asked Jennifer.

"Of course we did," laughed Caycee. "It was funny to us."

"Then that's why they didn't believe you."

"I know...but we couldn't help it," replied Miranda. "I would never have dreamed there was anyone else in the world that looks like me. After Mom died, I thought that was it."

"One day you may have a little girl who looks like you," responded Caycee.

"I would love to have a baby and I wouldn't care who he/she looked like," replied Miranda. "Enough of this talk; I had better help Jennifer with supper."

"What do you mean, HELP?" asked Jennifer. "I thought you were cooking."

"Not tonight, my dear sister," responded Miranda. "We're doing it together this time."

"Okay, I guess I can help you," teased Jennifer.

"Let me take my packages upstairs and hide them in the closet so Mardi won't find them. I want to surprise him tonight. I'll be back down to help you with dinner."

"Make sure you do," laughed Jennifer.

Miranda was only gone a few minutes, then came bounding down the stairs. She was in a bubbly mood and Jennifer was happy to see her this way. It had been a long time since she had seemed this happy. "Where's Caycee?" she asked.

"She said she was going to rest until dinner time."

"Good," replied Jennifer. "That will give us a chance to talk."

"About what?"

"About your change of attitude toward Caycee, that's what!" exclaimed Jennifer.

"Oh, that." laughed Miranda. "We had a little talk on the way to Billings this morning. I told her exactly how I felt about her flirting with Mardi and she apologized and said it would never happen again. She said she was only having fun."

"Yes, at your expense!" exclaimed Jennifer. "I think she could find a better way to have fun. I think you still need to keep your eyes open!"

"She promised she wouldn't do it anymore."

"How well do we know this girl? True, she is our cousin and we'd like to think she can be trusted, but I would be cautious."

"Okay, big sister and my protector... I will keep my eyes open."

"That's my girl. Sometimes I think you are too trusting. I'm just looking out for you because I love you."

"I thank you for being such a wonderful big sister, Jennifer. I don't know what I would do without you!"

"You know I'll always be here for you, Miranda! If anyone messes with you, they're messing with me. Don't you ever forget that!"

"Thanks, Jennifer and I love you!" exclaimed Miranda.

Chapter 11

The days passed and Caycee was true to her word. She behaved like a lady. This brought relief to Miranda and Jennifer. In fact, she asked if she could help them around the house, which was a surprise. She even wanted to cook dinner for all of them one night. So the girls turned the kitchen over to her. Both of them were anxious to see what kind of meal she would prepare. To their surprise she had a wonderful meal. They had no idea she could cook so well.

"Caycee, you have out done yourself," remarked Jennifer. "It must run in the blonde haired women."

"Thanks, Jennifer and why is that?" she asked.

"Well, seeing that you and Miranda are good cooks and I'm not is reason enough for me to believe it," she laughed. "Our mother was a great cook, also."

"So was mine!" exclaimed Caycee.

"Too bad I wasn't born blonde," suggested Jennifer.

"Don't sell yourself short, my dear sister," said Miranda. "You are a wonderful doctor and that is something none of us can do. So you see we are all different."

"I guess you are right, Miranda," laughed Jennifer. "As long as you are here to cook for us, at least I know my husband won't go hungry."

"Like that would happen!" exclaimed Miranda.

The guys came in from their work and washed up for

dinner. They all sat down and Gabe said the blessing. He thanked God for the food and for their wonderful, loving family. He was so thankful for Jennifer and Isabelle. They were his life. He missed Isac very much, but knew he was in Heaven with Jesus. He knew God had plans for him and needed him more than they did. Some people might think he had a strange way of thinking, but he felt so humble before God and would never question HIM on anything that happened. He knew that God NEVER makes a mistake, so therefore he couldn't question HIM on why HE took Isac so young. He knew that God had a purpose in it. That made him more determined to live for Jesus so he could go to Heaven and see Isac again. He was deep in thought when Jennifer interrupted his train of thoughts...

"Hey guys...Caycee cooked for us tonight!" exclaimed Jennifer.

"Oh really?" asked Gabe. "You've been holding out on us, huh?"

"Not really. I didn't want to come in here and take over."

"I don't mind sharing the kitchen with you," added Miranda. "I'll take all the help I can get."

"The food is delicious, Caycee," remarked Gabe. "It's almost as good as Miranda's." He was smiling as he teased her.

"Thank you, Gabe," Caycee said with a smile. "It means a lot to me."

Conversation was flowing as they all sat around the table. This was quality family time. It was about time that things returned to normal. The past couple of weeks had been very stressful, especially for Miranda. Jennifer didn't like to see her sister stressed. She couldn't help but remember all that Miranda had gone through with their dad's death. She was just now bouncing back and Jennifer was determined she was not going to stand by and let anyone hurt her sister.

Gabe looked at Jennifer and asked, "Have you heard any more from your friend in New York?"

"Matter of fact, I have," she replied. "I received an email from Harley today. He said he should be here in five days."

"Is he driving or flying?" asked Gabe.

"He's flying," said Jennifer.

"How long does he plan to stay?" asked Miranda.

"I'm not sure, but I don't think he will wear out his welcome!" Jennifer exclaimed. "It will be nice to see him again though. Ten years is a long time."

"I'm sure glad you never married him," teased Gabe.

"Me, too!" exclaimed Jennifer smiling. "Harley and I were only friends, Gabe. You don't have anything to worry about."

"That's good to know, Jennifer."

"You're the one and only one that I truly have loved all my life!"

"I sure am glad to hear that," he teased.

"Is this Harley guy married?" asked Caycee with delight.

"No, I don't think so, although he actually didn't say."

Well, then...I am looking forward to meeting him!" she exclaimed. "At this point in time, I am glad you and Miranda already have husbands."

"We are too!" exclaimed Miranda.

"Yes, Gabe and I are spoken for and that's the way it will remain the rest of our lives, right Gabe?" stated Mardi.

"Of course, Mardi. We are so blessed to be married to the prettiest girls in town," he said smiling.

"You can say that again!" exclaimed Gabe.

"Oh, that is so sweet, guys!" exclaimed Miranda.

"Count your blessings!" exclaimed Jennifer laughing.

"Well, maybe I will luck up and be exactly what Harley is looking for," laughed Caycee. "I just hope he isn't already attached."

"Actually, he never said anything about a wife or girlfriend when we talked," said Jennifer. "It seems as if he would have told me, had he been married."

"Oh, well...my luck is that he will already be married," said Caycee. "All the good ones are already taken." At this point she turned and looked at Mardi. The look never went unnoticed by Miranda. She was still keeping an eye on Caycee, even though she had apologized to her earlier.

They finished dinner and the guys retired to the den to talk over their days work. The girls cleaned up the kitchen and did the dishes before joining the guys in the den.

"I'm sure glad tomorrow is Sunday," stated Miranda. "I look forward to going to church. Are you going with us, Caycee?"

"I have been thinking about it," she responded. "I would like to experience that part of your life, too."

"That's great," replied Miranda. "Church is so important to all of us. We're all Christians and that makes our bond as a family even more special."

"Somehow, I envy you!" exclaimed Caycee. "I never really had anyone who cared that much about me."

"We're your family now...you have us!" exclaimed Miranda. "I'm so glad that you came to us. Otherwise, we would never have known you existed."

Sunday morning came and what a beautiful morning it was. The sun was shining brightly and the birds were singing melodious songs. How could anyone not believe in God with all His glorious beauty surrounding everyone? It filled Miranda's soul with joy, just looking at nature and the wonderful things that God had made, which so many people took for granted. She was so thankful for the family that God had given her and was still praying for a miracle child. She so badly wanted to have a baby but so far it hadn't happened. She kept holding on to the thought...*WITH GOD ALL THINGS ARE POSSIBLE.* She knew it would happen in His time...if it was His will. Meanwhile, she continued to pray.

It was a few minutes before eleven o'clock when they walked in the church door. It had been a pleasant ride over to the church. Everyone was in a good mood, including Caycee. She seemed to be excited about going to church. Miranda and Jennifer had really been praying for her.

The pastor had a good sermon taken from ROMANS 6:23 (KJV) ***For the wages of sin is death; but the gift of God is eternal life through Jesus Christ our Lord.***

Caycee took in every word. When the altar call was given, she was the first one to head toward the front and fell down on her knees at the altar. Miranda was right behind her and knelt to pray with her. When they stood up, the tears were streaming down Caycee's face and Miranda could see a change in her. She had accepted Jesus as her Lord and Savior. Miranda was crying tears of joy also. Another lost sheep had been found. "Thank you, Jesus," she said to herself. They walked back to their seat, with an angelic smile on their faces.

There was great rejoicing among the family on the ride home. Everyone had a lifted spirit. Another family member had surrendered her life to the Lord. It had all worked out wonderfully. If Caycee hadn't come for a visit, she may never have accepted Jesus as her Savior. The timing was perfect...God does everything in HIS own time.

In the following days they all saw a difference in Caycee's actions. They all knew that only God could make such a drastic change in a person and were so thankful for what He had done. They also knew that it was in His plans that she would come visit them and be saved.

Chapter 12

The next few days passed quickly. Jennifer was at work when she received the call she had been waiting for. Harley Brock had arrived in Billings. She picked up her handbag and left her office and quickly headed to her car. She was so excited! She reminisced as she drove to the airport. Although she only knew Harley for a brief time in California, she really liked him. If she hadn't been so much in love with Gabe, something might have developed between her and Harley. There was no use dwelling on that idea, because she was deeply in love and had married her soul mate.

There he was…standing inside the airport watching for her. Jennifer ran up to him and they both entwined their arms. There was excitement in the air. She was hoping Harley wouldn't read anything in to this as she considered him as a good friend only.

"Hello, Jennifer!" exclaimed Harley. "You're just as beautiful as ever!"

"Why thank you, Harley," she responded. "It is so good to see you and you are looking great also."

He picked up his bags and they started walking toward her car. "I can't wait for you to meet my family," said Jennifer.

"I am very much looking forward to that! I'm also

excited about seeing the ranch. I've heard so much about it that I somehow feel like I have been there."

"It's almost like Heaven living there," stated Jennifer with a smile.

"So there are no regrets in leaving California?"

"NONE, whatsoever! I'm a country girl at heart!"

The drive back to the ranch seemed shorter than usual. They were so busy talking and trying to catch up and it made the ride shorter. "So, how long can you stay with us?" asked Jennifer.

"Oh, maybe a week or so," he replied.

"A week or so? That is not long enough to show you around!"

"I never told you where I'm heading. I wanted to wait and tell you in person. I am going back to California."

"TO CALIFORNIA?" asked Jennifer in an excited voice. "Why?"

"My dad is in poor health now and he wants me to take over the family business," stated Harley.

"Oh, I am so sorry!" exclaimed Jennifer. "What about your job with the newspaper in New York?"

"I have already quit my job."

"I am so sorry! You waited all those years for that job and I know it's hard to give it up."

"I did what I had to do. I never had a choice. My mom could not run the hardware store by herself, so I'm doing what any good son would do."

"I always said you were a wonderful man and now this proves it even more," she stated. "How is your mom?"

"She is doing fairly well for her age. She is so excited that I am coming back to help her," said Harley.

"I'm sure she is. She must be very proud of you!"

"Oh, I think she likes me a little bit," said Harley with

a grin. "She told me she would hire someone to help her, if I didn't want to leave New York."

"She sounds like a wonderful mom!"

"Oh, she is...indeed she is."

"Make the most of the time you have with her and your Dad. Speaking from experience, it is NEVER the same once Mom and Dad are gone," stated Jennifer.

"I'm sure you're right. I am so sorry that you had to give yours up so soon."

"Thanks. Me, too! Sometime life seems so unfair. I had a really rough time when we lost Isac."

"Bless your heart, my dear Jennifer...you have been through so much."

"I'm so thankful I have God in my life or I would never have made it through this. Even then it was very hard."

"I just can't imagine... How old is Isabelle now?"

"She's seven and quite a young lady."

"Well, I can't wait to meet her!" exclaimed Harley. "If she's anything like her mother, then she has to be beautiful!"

"Oh, thank you, Harley. You are a very special friend!"

"For the short time we knew each other, we sure formed a bond, didn't we? Just suppose there had been no Gabe and I hadn't gone to New York...Do you think there would ever have been anything between us?"

"Yes, I think there could have been. I really liked you a lot and still do, but Gabe captured my heart many, many years ago," she added smiling.

"I know he did...I could tell by the way you talked to him that night on the phone so many years ago. Jennifer, I honestly am happy that things worked out for the two of you. Gabe is one lucky man!"

"Thank you, Harley. Only those words could come from a very honest friend."

"I guess I just got there too late," he said teasing her. "I keep hoping there is someone special out there for me, too."

"Oh, I feel sure there is. You need to wait on God and not rush it. Sometimes we try to take things into our own hands and that is when we mess up. Trust me, I have been there."

They pulled into the driveway of the ranch house. "This is a beautiful place, Jennifer!" exclaimed Harley. "I can see why you wanted to move back here and get away from California!"

"This is the only place I would ever want to be. I guess you can't take the country out of the girl. My mother loved this placed so much..." she said with sad eyes.

"I know that had to be rough and I am so sorry, Jennifer!"

"I have to keep living and try not to dwell on the past. Sometimes it really hits me hard though."

"I'm sure it does. I still have my mom, so I really don't know how it feels."

"Well, we're home, so we'd better get inside and get you introduced to the family. They're all anxiously waiting. I didn't tell you that we have other company also. I thought I'd surprise you," said Jennifer with a laugh.

"Male or female?" he asked smiling.

"You'll have to wait and see," remarked Jennifer as they got out of the car. As they were walking up the steps the door opened and there stood Miranda.

"I think I've died and gone to Heaven!" exclaimed Harley. "This must be an angel!"

"Meet my sister, Miranda," said Jennifer. "Miranda, this is Harley Brock."

The two exchanged handshakes and greetings. Jennifer was hoping Miranda hadn't heard Harley's remark. She was sure she would hear about it if she had. She and Miranda were very close and open with everything. It was so good to have such a close relationship with her sister. She knew they were blessed to have each other.

"Let's go inside and meet the others," said Jennifer to Harley. She could hear voices in the den and knew that Gabe and Mardi were there. She was glad. They walked into the den and the two guys rose to their feet. "Gabe... Mardi...I'd like for you to meet an old friend of mine from California. This is Harley Brock."

"Nice to finally meet you, Harley!" exclaimed Gabe extending his hand. "Jennifer has been singing your praises ever since she knew you were coming for a visit."

"Is that so?" laughed Harley as he glanced at Jennifer. "As good as that sounds, YOU are the one she has always been in love with. I knew that from the first time she mentioned your name. I am happy for you, Gabe and it is finally good to get to meet you."

"Thank you," said Gabe. "Now, I feel more at ease with you being here. We're glad you came and you're welcome to stay as long as you wish."

"Thanks, Gabe and you have nothing to worry about. Jennifer and I have only been friends...even from the beginning."

"I'd like to welcome you, also," said Mardi extending his hand for a handshake. "As Gabe said...we've been hearing good things about you."

"Thank you, Mardi. I am assuming this beautiful blonde is your wife."

"You assumed correctly. Miranda is the love of my life!" exclaimed Mardi. "I fell in love with her the instant I saw her, but she never knew it for quite awhile."

"I can see why," remarked Harley as he turned and looked at Miranda. "She is indeed a beautiful woman!" He turned and looked directly at Jennifer and said, "So are you, Jennifer. Both of you are very beautiful! Gabe and Mardi are two very lucky men!"

"Thank you," responded the girls in unison. "I feel like we're the lucky ones," said Jennifer.

About this time Isabelle entered the room. Harley knelt down in front of her and took her hand and kissed it. "This must be the beautiful little Isabelle!" he exclaimed.

"Indeed it is," replied Jennifer. "Isabelle, say hello to my friend, Harley."

Looking a little shy after the kiss, she said, "Hi Harley."

"Well...hello, Isabelle. You're a beautiful little girl and look just like your Mother."

"You think so?" she asked in excitement.

"I do...," replied Harley.

"May I be excused?" asked Isabelle looking at her Mother.

"Of course, dear. I'll call you when it's dinner time."

"Thanks, Mom," she answered as she ran up the stairs.

"Is there someone else I need to meet?" asked Harley with suspense. "I think you told me you had a house guest."

"Yes, I did, Harley. Just a minute..."

Jennifer walked over to the stairs and yelled, "CAYCEE...can you come downstairs?"

A few minutes later Caycee descended the stairs, dressed in a bright red, off the shoulder, sheath dress. She was a beautiful sight to behold! Her beautiful, long, golden hair was a cascade of curls flowing down her back. All eyes were fixed upon her...Harley's mouth dropped open and he could hardly speak. "You've got to be kidding me," he said to Jennifer. "Where have you been hiding this Goddess? You didn't tell me that you had twin sisters. She looks just like Miranda!"

"Actually, she is our first cousin, Caycee Canfield. Her mother and our mother were identical twins. Miranda and Caycee happen to look like their mothers."

Harley walked over and met Caycee as she stepped off the last step. He extended his hand to her and as she accepted, he kissed her hand. "Just who is this gentleman?" asked Caycee with a sweet smile.

"This is my friend, Harley Brock, from New York, who is on his way back to his original home in California. He decided to stop by to see us on the way."

"Nice to meet you, Harley, and welcome to the ranch. I haven't been here long myself. I wanted to meet my cousins before going to Paris."

"Paris??? What takes you to Paris?" he asked.

"Oh, I'm a fashion designer and I have a show in Paris in less than two months."

"I find that very interesting," said Harley. "As you descended the stairs I told myself that you looked like a model, so I guess I was right."

"I don't actually model...I make the designs. This dress is one of my designs."

"As I see it, you should also be modeling your designs!"

"Thank you, Harley, but I don't have time for both. It keeps me busy creating my designs."

"Well, you sure are talented, my dear!"

"Thanks, Harley. I love what I do. This is my life."

"You mean there is no man in your life?" asked Harley with pleasure.

"Not at the present," Caycee responded. "I really don't have much time for a relationship."

"That's too bad," he teased. "Here I am and I'm available..."

"I see...I'm surprised you're not already married. It seems all the good ones are already taken."

"There's still a few of us around...waiting for the right woman to come along," he said smiling at her. "Would you like to have dinner with me one night this week?"

Caught off guard, Caycee hesitated for a few seconds, "Boy, you don't waste any time, do you?" she asked laughing.

"When I see something I want, I go after it. Most of the time you lose by putting off things."

"Is that so?" she asked with a laugh. "Harley, I would be delighted to have dinner with you."

"GREAT! How about tomorrow night?"

"Tomorrow night would be fine," she responded. "I'll be looking forward to it."

"Me, too!" he exclaimed with a big boyish grin. He looked at Jennifer who gave him a thumbs up. He was really glad he had decided to stop by the ranch and see Jennifer. Little did he know that this was going to change his future.

Chapter 13

Miranda was happy that Harley had 'eyes' for Caycee. This somehow eased her mind about Caycee. Even though she had gotten saved, there was still a part of Miranda that didn't trust her. Now that Harley was here, she was hoping Caycee would really get involved with him and forget all about Mardi. She just needed her life back to normal.

For the past week she hadn't been feeling well. She didn't know if it was something she ate or what. She hadn't mentioned it to anyone. She hated to complain so much. She'd had her share of sickness and troubles in the past year. She was trying her best to act normal for Mardi. He had been through a lot with her since they had gotten married.

Another week passed and she was still feeling queasy at her stomach. Then it hit her...could I be pregnant? She knew there was a very good chance she could be. She went to check the calendar to see when her last monthly period was. To her surprise, she was two weeks late. A smile crossed her face and then she chuckled. This is what she and Mardi had been praying for. She decided to take an EPT before telling Mardi. She didn't want to build up his hopes, only to have them dashed if she wasn't pregnant.

The next morning she left the house with plans to do some grocery shopping. Little did they know she had other things on her mind. She stopped in at the pharmacy first thing and bought the test, then proceeded on to the grocery store. She decided to cook a special dinner tonight for her family. She knew that Caycee was going out with Harley, so it would just be their immediate family. She was happy about that, just in case...she had some good news to share with them.

After she got back home she put all the groceries away, and then slipped off to the bathroom. She couldn't wait to get the results of the EPT. She knelt down on her knees beside the tub and poured her heart out to God. "Dear God," she prayed. "Please let the test be positive. You know how much Mardi and I want to have a baby. If it's in your will for us to have a baby, I promise... I will be the best mother ever and will raise my baby in church and teach him or her the ways of the Lord. Thank you, God! In Jesus name I pray. Amen."

She got up and wiped the tears from her eyes. She knew God had heard her prayer...

She proceeded to do the test and sat down to wait. "Thank you, God!" she shouted as she saw the test was positive. "I'M PREGNANT!" she yelled as she ran down the stairs. There was no one in the house to hear her. Caycee had gone riding earlier. Miranda had met her heading toward the stable as she pulled into the driveway. Since there's no one here now, I'll wait and tell everyone at dinner she decided. She didn't know how she would get through lunch with Mardi, Gabe and Caycee, but she sure was going to try. She wanted Jennifer to be here when she shared the wonderful news.

She fixed soup and sandwiches for lunch and everyone seemed to enjoy it. Miranda tried to act as normal as she could. The guys were talking mostly ranch talk, for which Miranda was glad. Caycee was all excited about her date with Harley. Miranda joined in both conversations and was glad no one asked her where she had been.

The afternoon passed quickly and Miranda was on top of the world. She could hardly wait for dinner time to get here and have everyone gathered around the table. She would then spring the BIG NEWS on them.

Harley arrived back at the house at 5:00 p.m. He had been in Billings for the day. When he arrived, he was carrying a bouquet of flowers. Caycee was in the den when he arrived.

"Where's Caycee?" he asked as he entered the house.

"I think she's in the den," replied Miranda.

"Thanks," added Harley as he walked toward the den.

"Hi Caycee." He walked over and gave her a brief hug. "These are for you," he said as he handed her the beautiful bouquet of red roses.

She took them and gasped. "These are very beautiful! Thank you so much, Harley!"

"Beautiful roses for a beautiful lady," he explained with a smile.

"Thank you, Harley. You've just made my day!"

"I'm hoping to make the rest of your day good, too. Are you ready to go?"

"Yes," she said as she followed him out of the den. They went out the back door saying goodbye to Miranda on the way out.

Miranda had dinner ready by six o'clock. Jennifer was home from the office and the guys were in from their work. "Dinner's ready."

Jennifer and Isabelle came down the steps in a hurry. "I'm starving," said Isabelle.

"Good," said Miranda. "I love to feed you when you're hungry."

They all took their place around the table and Gabe said the blessing. After he finished, Miranda spoke up. "Before we eat, I have something special to share with all of you! As you know, I have not been feeling well for the past few weeks. Well, now...there seems to be a reason for that. I'M PREGNANT!!!"

Mardi jumped up from his chair and grabbed Miranda in a big hug. "Are you sure?" he asked excitedly. "Have you been to the doctor? Why didn't you tell me?" He was full of questions.

"Yes, I am sure. I bought an EPT and it was positive. I didn't tell you because I wanted to be sure before I told anyone."

"This is such exciting news, Miranda!" exclaimed Jennifer. "That's just what we need...another baby in the house! I am so happy for you both!!!"

"I'm going to be a DADDY! Thank you GOD!!!" exclaimed Mardi. "This is the second best day of my life!"

"SECOND?" inquired Miranda looking puzzled.

"Yes, second. The BEST day was when I married YOU!!!"

"Oh, I guess I never thought of that," she responded.

"CONGRATULATIONS!!! I wish you both the best!!!" exclaimed Gabe. "You'll make wonderful parents!"

"Thank you," said Miranda and Mardi in unison.

They ate their dinner with joy filling the air. Each one felt it. They were such a close family and rejoiced with each other when there was happiness. They also wept with each other in times of sorrow.

Meanwhile, Harley and Caycee were having a wonderful time. He took her to an elegant restaurant in

Billings. After they ate, they sat and talked a long time. There was magic in the air and both of them felt it.

"I hate for this night to end," said Harley. "It has been wonderful! You are terrific to be with."

"Thank you, Harley! I've had a wonderful time!"

"Do you want to go out again tomorrow night?" he asked smiling.

"Sure." After all, being with him made her happy. "How long are you going to be here?"

"Oh, I don't want to think about that right now. I will probably stay for a week, and then I need to move on to California. My parents are expecting me soon."

"I wish you didn't have to go so soon!"

"You could always go with me," he added with a surprising grin.

"WHAT?" she gasped. "You know I can't do that. I have to go to Paris in a few weeks."

"You could go with me and stay until your Paris trip."

"Aren't you rushing things?" she asked. "What would your parents say?"

"We have a guest room where you could stay. I am not asking you to go 'live' with me! My parents would be fine with it, as long as you sleep in the guest room."

"I'll have to think about it," she sighed...

"You have one week, then I will need an answer."

"Okay, Harley," she answered with a smile. In her heart she already knew the answer.

The week passed quickly and it was time for Harley to leave. He had enjoyed his visit so much. He and Caycee had gone out to dinner every night. He was hoping she would say 'yes' in answer to his question about her going to California with him for a few weeks. On their last night he finally got up the nerve to ask her. "Well, Caycee...

have you made a decision to the question I asked you a few days ago?"

"Harley, I like you very much but our timing seems to be off at the present. If I didn't have this trip ahead of me, I would go with you. Believe me, I am tempted! I really need to concentrate on this project and make sure it goes off without a hitch. I don't think I would take the time to do what I need to do if I went home with you. So for now, I am going to have to say 'no' to you. Maybe sometime in the future I can pay you a visit, that is, if the invitation still stands."

"Of course, the invitation still stands. Let's put it this way, you have an open invitation. I must say I sure am disappointed you can't go now, but I do understand. If we are meant to have a future together, I know God will work everything out."

"You're very correct," said Caycee. "It's all in God's hands. I am so thankful that I came to know Jesus as my personal Savior."

"Me, too!" exclaimed Harley. "I wouldn't want to go one day without God in my life!"

"You know…I have thought about this many times since I got saved. If I hadn't come to the ranch and met these wonderful Christian cousins of mine, I might never have become a Christian. That is frightening to think about. The sad thing is…I didn't realize that I was a sinner and on the road to hell."

Harley left the next day and a few tears were shed as they parted ways. It had been a wonderful week for both him and Caycee. He was looking forward to seeing her again one day.

Jennifer had invited him back to the ranch anytime that he could get away from California. He was so glad to have a friend like Jennifer. She held a special place in his heart. He was also glad that he got to meet her wonderful family. They were very special people! Maybe someday he could come back for another visit. Maybe...just maybe, if things worked out for him and Caycee, he would be part of this family. This thought brought a smile to his face. He would pray about it and leave it in God's hands.

Chapter 14

Miranda made an appointment with an OB/GYM, Dr. Cody Morgan. He had only been in Billings for three years, but Jennifer highly recommended him. She told Miranda that she had heard many good things about him. So Miranda took Jennifer's word and made the doctor appointment. She was so happy that Gabe was able to spare Mardi that day so he could go with her. She would feel better knowing her loving husband was by her side. She was somewhat nervous anyway. She had wanted a baby for quite a long while and was afraid she might not be pregnant, even though the EPT said she was. She asked God to calm her nerves and give her the baby she longed for.

The day of the appointment, she felt at ease and gave God the thanks. Everything went smoothly and soon the doctor gave them the good news they had been hoping to hear. "Miranda," Dr. Morgan spoke softly, "You and Mardi are going to have a baby in about seven months. You are two months pregnant."

The tears flowed from Miranda's eyes. "I'm sorry, Dr. Morgan, I am just so happy!"

"I understand Miranda and you don't owe me an apology. I am happy to bring you such good news. Everything looks fine and I see no reason why you shouldn't have a normal, healthy pregnancy. I'll start you on some pre-natal vitamins and I'll see you in one month."

"Thank you, doctor!" she exclaimed with a smile.

"Thanks, Dr. Morgan," said Mardi as the two guys shook hands.

They left his office so excited. Both had big smiles on their face and anyone could tell they had gotten good news. They could hardly wait to tell their families. Mardi planned to call his family on Prince Edward Island before nightfall.

This would change things on the ranch. Recently, Miranda had been talking about looking for a part-time job at a vet clinic. Mardi was sure that wouldn't happen, at least not for a few years. He was thinking about this and suddenly he had a brilliant idea. They hadn't reached home yet, so he decided to approach Miranda with his crazy idea. "Miranda, I was just thinking...I guess this will put a halt on your plans for looking for work, right?"

"I suppose it will, Mardi."

"I was just thinking...."

"Just what were you thinking, Mardi?" she asked wondering what was on his mind.

"I know you love working with animals and you are so good with them. I was thinking... how would you like to have your very own vet clinic...here on the ranch?"

"What? Are you crazy, Mardi?" she asked in surprise. "How could we do that?"

"I think we could build you a clinic with a nursery for the baby, so you could take him or her with you every day. We can hire someone to help with the baby also."

"Mardi, where did you come up with such an idea?" she asked in awe.

"I just want you to be happy, my darling Miranda!"

"Well, after the shock…I think it's a brilliant idea!" she exclaimed with a big smile.

"I'm glad you like the idea. I will talk to Gabe about this and we'll try to get all the details worked out and draw a floor plan for the clinic. Of course you'll be the one to make the final decision on the floor plans. I want to build it exactly like you want it."

"Oh, Mardi," she said with tears in her eyes, "You are the best!"

"Thank you, Miranda. I just love you so much and want to make you happy…especially now that you're going to be a mommy," he added with a loving smile.

"That is so sweet of you and I know you're going to make a wonderful daddy!"

"I'll give it my best shot," he added proudly. "You know if we get started right away on your clinic it should be ready to open by the time you are ready to go to work after our baby is born."

"That sounds wonderful! I am so excited!"

"I'll talk to Gabe tonight and begin making plans."

She looked at him as he was driving and said, "I love you so much, Mardi Carson. How did I ever make it without you?"

"I love you very much, my dear Miranda, and I don't know how I ever made it before you came into my life!"

That night at the dinner table Mardi brought up the subject of a new vet clinic. Gabe was surprised but had nothing to say against it. In fact he thought it was a good idea. That way Miranda would be able to work at something she loved and also be with her baby.

"I think it's a brilliant idea!" exclaimed Jennifer. "I can tell all my patients and get you lots of referrals, Miranda. I'm sure about all of my patients have animals."

"Thanks, Jennifer. That would be a great way to get

word around. I'm sure after the word is out I will have all the work I can do. Most people treat their animals just like humans."

"That is good...especially for you," laughed Jennifer. "I think you will be a success, Miranda."

"I sure hope so."

Caycee had been silent most of the meal. She finally added, "I wish you the best, Miranda."

"Thanks, Caycee. Maybe by the time you come back for a visit the clinic will be open."

"I hope so. I look forward to visiting again sometime. This has been nice but my time is almost up. I will be leaving in a few days, heading to Paris."

"We all wish you the best, Caycee!" exclaimed Miranda. "You need to keep in touch with us and let us know how things are going for you. We will keep you in our daily prayers!"

"Thank you," said Caycee. "I know I'm going to need it."

Three days later Miranda drove her to the airport and watched her board the plane heading for New York. From there she would be heading to Paris. Miranda hoped that all would go well for Caycee and prayed that she wouldn't forget God in the midst of all this glory. She also hoped Caycee would keep in touch with them. Time would tell...

Chapter 15

Meanwhile, life was back to normal on the ranch. The house seemed much quieter with Caycee gone. She had definitely left a mark on the Parker Ranch!

Mardi, along with Miranda's guidance, had drawn the plans for the new clinic. It was well on its way now. Things had gone so smoothly for which Mardi was thankful. Miranda was so excited! In fact, she had more than that to be excited about. She was going to have a baby in five months. She was getting along fine and was going to have an ultrasound on her next doctor's visit. She and Mardi had decided they wanted to know what they were having. That way she could prepare the nursery in the house and the clinic.

Two weeks passed. Miranda woke up to the sun streaming through the blinds in her bedroom window. She heard a songbird chirping in a nearby tree. He sounded so joyful and yet it was so early in the morning or so she thought. She reached over and lay her arm on the empty pillow next to her. Mardi had already gotten up and left her to sleep in. She collected her thoughts and jumped out of bed. Today was her doctor appointment. Had Mardi forgotten? She grabbed her robe and flew downstairs. No one was in sight. Her appointment was less than three hours away. She had to find Mardi...

She slipped on her boots and headed toward the barn.

She could hear voices so maybe she would find Mardi. Several of the cowboys were cleaning out the stalls and putting in fresh hay. They never noticed Miranda as she entered the barn. "Hello." she shouted.

"Hello, Miranda," said one of the guys named Jude. "What can we do for you?"

"Have you seen Mardi?" she asked in panic.

"Yes, he was here earlier. I think he has gone with Gabe to check the fences."

"Oh my goodness," she sighed.

"What's the matter?' asked Jude.

"I have a doctor appointment in a few hours and Mardi is supposed to go with me. I'm having an ultrasound today to determine the sex of the baby," she added with a big smile.

"I'm sure he will be back in time. I don't think he would forget something that important," Jude said with a laugh.

"I sure hope you're right, Jude! I sure would hate to leave without him! If you see him when he gets back, will you tell him to come to the house immediately?"

"I sure will."

"Thanks, Jude!"

"Anytime, Miranda!" he exclaimed. He turned and went back to work as Miranda exited the barn.

Half an hour later Mardi entered the house. Miranda was in her room dressing as he came bounding up the stairs. "I'm sorry I'm late," he said to Miranda. "Gabe and I just finished checking about half of the fences. We'll try to get the rest tomorrow."

"You still have time to get ready," she replied. "I sure am glad you made it in time."

"You know I wouldn't let you down, Miranda!" he exclaimed. "I told Gabe I had to be back in time to go with you, so here I am!" With outstretched arms he came to give her a big hug and kiss. "I love you, Miranda!"

"I love you, too, Mardi! Thank you for being such a wonderful, understanding husband!"

"Oh, Miranda...you make it so easy!"

Two hours later they were walking out of the doctor's office with a big smile gracing their faces. "I am still in awe of our baby!" Mardi exclaimed. "Watching the video made it seem so much more real. I am very happy that we are having a baby girl. I hope she looks just like her mommy!"

"Oh, Mardi...you are so sweet! I hope you're not disappointed that we're not having a boy. I know all men want a son."

"I am not disappointed in the least. Maybe the next one will be a boy," he teased.

"Whoa...let me get through this one first, and then we'll talk about the boy."

"You know I'm teasing," he added. "If it's God's will for us to have two children, then I won't care if the second one is another girl. God knows what is best for us."

"You are so right," replied Miranda as she got into the car. "I think I'll call Jennifer. I can't wait until she gets home."

"Sure, go ahead."

"Hi Jennifer, it's Miranda."

"Well, what kind of good news do you have for me?" asked an excited Jennifer.

"We're having a baby GIRL!!! I am so happy!"

"Congratulations!" exclaimed Jennifer. "Now Isabelle will have a playmate!"

"I know...won't that be great? They can grow up like sisters!"

"I know Isabelle will be so excited to hear the news," said Jennifer. "I can't wait to tell her."

That night at dinner, Miranda and Mardi shared their good news with Gabe and Isabelle. As Mardi said the blessing, he thanked God for his wonderful wife and for the unborn baby she was carrying. He asked God's blessing on both of them. He had learned so much about God from this wonderful woman he had married. He gave her credit for guiding him in the right way.

Isabelle was very excited..."Aunt Miranda, I am so happy you are going to get a baby girl. Then I will have someone to play with," she beamed.

"I'm glad you are happy, Isabelle! She can be like a little sister to you."

"I know..." thought Isabelle for a moment. "I hope she looks like me."

"We'll have to wait and see on that one," laughed Miranda. "I have a feeling she is going to have blonde hair."

"I want her to have dark hair like me!" exclaimed Isabelle.

"My dear little niece...I'm afraid we have no control over that. God is making her right now and He knows exactly what color hair He is going to give her."

"Oh well...," sighed Isabelle. "I'll take her no matter who she looks like."

"That's my girl!" exclaimed Jennifer. "She will love you as a big sister and that's all that matters."

"I guess," sighed Isabelle.

After dinner was over and the kitchen was clean, Miranda called her brothers Rob, Jordan and Blake. They were all excited and wished her the best. She was so happy that she was finally pregnant. God had blessed her with this pregnancy and she promised Him that she would dedicate her baby to Him. She had such a strong faith in God. He had brought her through many trials in the past few years. Thinking back she realized she could never have made it if it hadn't been for her faith and belief in the Lord. He certainly had seen her through some trying times.

The next several months went by without any problems for Miranda. She gave God all the praise for this. She knew she and her baby were in His hands and she never worried about her pregnancy. She knew HE would take care of her! She and Mardi had discussed names for the baby and both had agreed on Taylor. They were anxiously awaiting her arrival.

The long awaited day finally came. At 3:00 a.m. on Sunday morning, Miranda woke up Mardi. "It's time!" she exclaimed. "We'd better get to the hospital."

Mardi jumped out of bed and quickly put on his clothes. "Are you sure?" he asked in a half awake voice.

"Yes, Mardi...I am SURE! Please get the overnight bag I have packed and I will start getting dressed."

"Sure thing," he answered excitedly.

After Miranda got dressed she went to knock on Jennifer's bedroom door. "Jennifer," she called quietly. No answer..."Jennifer," she called a little louder. This time she heard the creaking of the bed. She knew Jennifer was getting up.

The door opened and a half asleep Jennifer appeared. "Are you okay?" she asked.

"Yes, I'm fine," beamed Miranda. "I am about to have a baby!"

"A baby!" squealed Jennifer. "What can I do to help?"

"You can come to the hospital if you want to. Mardi and I are about ready to leave."

"I'll be there as quickly as I can, Miranda. You know I want to be there with you!"

"I know and I appreciate you, my dear sister!"

"I know you do," replied Jennifer. "Go...my little sister and have us a baby girl."

"I'll do my best. We had better get on the road. The pains are getting closer."

"Go now, and may God be with you," Jennifer added.

Five hours later, seven pound, four ounce, Taylor Lynn Carson made her entrance into the world. She had a head full of blonde hair and eyes as blue as the sky. She had a little round face and dimples in her cheeks. She was a beautiful baby!

Miranda and Mardi were in awe of their baby daughter. They felt so blessed that God had given them this beautiful little baby to raise. At this moment they felt they were the luckiest couple in the world. They had waited so long for this baby, but knew that she belonged to God...He had let them borrow her for awhile. No matter if her life was short or long, she belonged to God and they prayed they would never forget.

Taylor Lynn Carson...TLC...stands for Tender Loving Care. That was exactly what Miranda and Mardi intended to give their baby daughter. God had given them this precious jewel to take care of and they would.

Miranda and baby Taylor came home from the hospital two days later. Everyone was all excited, especially Isabelle. She could hardly wait to hold baby Taylor. They started bonding from the very first day.

Miranda was sitting on the sofa and seemed to be in another world. "Is anything wrong?" asked Jennifer.

"Nooooo, not really," replied Miranda. "I was just thinking..."

"About what?" asked her sister.

"About Mom and Dad. I was thinking how happy they would be. I wish they were here to see baby Taylor."

"Me, too! One day when we all go to Heaven, we can see Mom and Dad and little Isac again."

"I know...that will be a wonderful day, won't it?"

"It sure will," replied Jennifer. "I miss my baby boy so much!"

"I know you do, Jennifer. I just can't imagine giving up a child!"

"No one knows the pain unless they have been through it!" exclaimed Jennifer wiping her tears. "It's the worst thing I've ever been through."

"I am sooo sorry!" exclaimed Miranda. "I wish it had never happened, but God had a purpose in it. We may never know the reason, but we can be assured that God NEVER makes a mistake."

"I know and that is the only way I can deal with it. The fact that we will be reunited again someday is the only thought I can hold on to."

Later that evening Jordan, Haley and their daughter came over from Billings for a visit. They decided to wait until she got home from the hospital before visiting. They brought a beautiful bouquet of flowers for Miranda and a gift for the baby. It was the most angelic little white dress that Miranda had ever seen. It was covered with lace and ribbons. She knew right away this would be the dress her baby would wear when she was dedicated at church. There was also a matching sweater and blanket.

There were flowers and gifts from Rob and Kati on Prince Edward Island and even from Blake in Hollywood. All of them were sending their congratulations and best wishes to Mom, Dad and the baby. The biggest surprise of all came later in the week. Miranda was very surprised when Fed-Ex delivered a big package that had come all the way from Paris! Caycee had outdone herself. She had everything you could imagine in the box for baby Taylor. When she saw another gift with her name on it, she was even more surprised. She carefully opened it and let out a gasp... Inside the box was the most beautiful silk dress she had ever seen. It was emerald green...Miranda's color... She read the name tag only to see it was from Caycee's line of clothes. She was so excited and surprised. She couldn't believe that Caycee had done this for her. She was so glad she had made friends with Caycee and led her to the Lord. She was indeed a different girl than she was the day she first arrived on the ranch. Miranda was so glad she never turned her back on her cousin.

Chapter 16

Baby Taylor Lynn was four months old when Jennifer made her BIG announcement. She came home from work one evening with a smile from ear to ear.

"You seem to be in a very good mood today, Jennifer!" exclaimed Miranda smiling as she seated herself at the dinner table.

"Indeed I am," replied Jennifer as she took her place at the table. "I have some news for all of you."

"Out with it!" exclaimed Miranda. "Don't keep us in suspense!"

"What would you say if I told you there is going to be another baby in our house?"

"A BABY???" shrieked Miranda. "What are you trying to tell us?"

"I'm telling you that Gabe and I are going to have another baby!" she exclaimed with a big grin.

"That's right," responded Gabe. "We are so happy with our news and wanted to share it with you as soon as we were sure."

"I went to the doctor today and he says I am two months pregnant."

"That is WONDERFUL news!" exclaimed Miranda. "Taylor will have a little cousin to grow up with. Isabelle will have her hands full with two babies, won't she?"

"She sure will," laughed Jennifer. "I'm sure she will love every minute of it."

"I can't wait to have a little brother or sister!" chimed in Isabelle with a huge smile.

* * * * * * * * * * * *

Miranda's clinic, M & M ANIMAL CLINIC, had been open for a month. She decided on that name because hers and Mardi's first name began with an M. She was really enjoying being back to work, especially since she could take Taylor with her. She had hired a girl in her early thirties as a nanny to help care for Taylor during the day. She was very good with Taylor and took the best of care of her. It put Miranda's mind at ease when she saw how good the new nanny was with the baby. Ellie Livingston seemed to be a Godsend.

Business was picking up as word was getting around. She was doing very little advertising. Word of mouth was always better, she thought. She had other ranchers who were bringing their animals to her instead of going into town. It was closer for them and was giving Miranda a chance also. She was grateful for this. Sometimes she made 'house calls' to the ranches when they had a sick horse or cow. She never turned anyone down. She was doing what she loved to do. She was such a caregiver of humans and animals.

Miranda wanted to thank all her customers for their support, so she decided to have a big cook-out for them. She put together a list of people who had been there in the past month, plus a few others and sent out the invitations. It had been a long time since they'd had a party on the ranch. She was really looking forward to this. Jennifer helped her with the menu and the guys were going to prepare the meat for pork barbeque. Jennifer was going to hire twin sisters, Ethel and Emily, to come in and cook the food for them. They had a small catering business, which they worked from their house in town. It was called '*Et & Em Catering*.' They agreed to come to the ranch and do the cooking since Jennifer and Miranda were busy with work. This would make things much easier for them. The sisters were happy to get the work. Both of them were widowed so they had plenty of time to help out, as their business didn't keep them busy all the time. After both their husbands passed on, the twins decided to combine households and found this was much cheaper on them. It brought back many memories of when they were growing up. They had always been close and this worked out perfect for them. They were in their early fifties and both loved to cook. They had many years of experience. In fact, they were said to be the best cooks in town. That's why Jennifer wanted them. Their reputation preceded them. They just happened to have that week available and Jennifer felt blessed that she was able to obtain them. They only had two weeks to get ready for this joyous occasion. Ethel and Emily were on standby...They had an older sister, Sallie, who helped them when they needed her. Sallie lived nearby so they kept a close eye on her. Her husband had left her for another woman and she dealt with depression quite often.

The main menu consisted of: Pork Barbeque, Potato Salad, Zesty Green Vegetables, BBQ Beans, Spicy Peanut Slaw, Fantastic Grilled Corn on the Cob, Buttery Spinach & Mushrooms, Cheesy Squash Casserole, Smoked Paprika Potato Wedges, Mediterranean Baked Spinach, Broccoli Casserole, Chicken Casserole, Macaroni Salad, Corn Muffins, Homemade Buttermilk Biscuits, Lemonade and Tea.

The dessert menu was: Old Fashioned Sweet Potato

Pie, Red Velvet Cup Cakes, Apple Cobbler, Cherry Cheesecake, Coconut Layer Cake, Peanut Butter Pie, Chocolate Eclair Cake, Butterscotch Pie, Peach Cobbler and Chocolate Chip Cookies.

After another week passed, Miranda and Jennifer went grocery shopping. They had gotten a list of ingredients from the sisters, who had carefully planned for each dish that they would prepare. With the SUV loaded, Jennifer and Miranda headed back to the ranch. They were getting very excited about the BBQ. It was so good knowing they didn't have to worry about the food. They knew Ethel and Emily would prepare each dish to perfection.

The sisters arrived around 8:30 a.m. on Monday morning. They didn't wait to be told what to do but started right away preparing the dishes that could be prepared a few days in advance. Miranda observed how well they worked together. She gave them her phone number at the clinic and told them to call if they needed her. The week went extremely well and the aroma in the kitchen was heavenly. Gabe and Mardi noticed this every evening when they came in from the field. They were always hungry and this made it especially hard for them. "Just a few more days," Miranda told them. "Then you can eat all you want."

"Some of it would taste good now," teased Mardi. "I know...I have to wait."

"I'm sorry, Mardi, but YES... you do have to wait!"

"Oh well," he said. "It's just two more days."

"That's right," added Gabe. "I'm going to see that you stay very busy those two days. We have a lot of work to do. We have to get all the tables and chairs set up. Don't forget, we are in charge of the barbeque."

"I know, I haven't forgotten," replied Mardi.

Everyone seemed to know their job and did it well.

Saturday afternoon came and everything was in order. Ethel and Emily had outdone themselves with the food. The tables and chairs were in place and they began carrying food to the long table which was covered with red and white plaid tablecloths. Everything looked so festive.

The crowd was beginning to gather. Miranda was expecting around one hundred people. They parked their cars in the field and walked to the picnic area. A line formed and they began to fill their plates with Ethel's and Emily's delicious food. There was so much joy in the air. Everyone seemed to be having a great time which really pleased Miranda. They all had worked so hard to make this day happen and seeing the guests having so much fun made it all worthwhile.

After everyone had finished eating, several women helped clean up while the children enjoyed some games. They played the sack race, dodge ball and many other games. The men sauntered off by themselves and talked about everything from hunting to ranching. They talked about branding cattle and taming wild mustangs. They never seemed to run out of things to talk about.

The tables were all cleared and the women had just sat down to rest and enjoy the remainder of the evening, but not for long.

About that time, there was the sound of dogs barking and a strange dog came running from behind the barn. Herman, Eddie and Lily were behind him. He was so fast it was hard for them to keep up with him. He seemed to be frightened. Miranda got out of her seat and called her dogs. Herman, Eddie and Lily came bounding to her. The other dog stopped and sat down a short distance away. He was a beautiful black lab and looked a lot like their ranch dogs. She continued to call him, but he never moved. He watched and listened. Miranda decided to walk toward him. Again, he never moved. When she got closer she started talking softly to him. He began to wag his tail. She ventured even closer and reached out her hand to him. He sniffed her hand then licked it and looked up at her with the saddest eyes she had ever seen. This melted her heart. "Come here boy," she said to him. He got up and came closer to her. She touched him on the head and he never moved. She saw that he was not wearing a collar. Who would have such a fine dog and not have a collar on him? She thought to herself. He was rather thin, which told her no one was taking care of him like they should. He looked very hungry and she knew it wouldn't be for long. She was going to feed him. So she continued to talk softly to him and he watched her very closely. "Come on boy," she said to him. "Let's go to the house and find you some food." She turned and started toward the house and he was right behind her. By this time Herman, Eddie and Lily saw them together and came running to join them. This time he never ran from them. They all acted like they knew him and he was supposed to be there with them. This pleased Miranda. Thoughts were running through her head..."This dog needs a home and we need him. If no one claims him, then he is ours."

The new dog ate like he was starved to death. Tears rolled down Miranda's face as she watched him. She was such a 'softie' where animals were concerned. After he seemed to be full, Miranda went back to join the ladies. "I guess you ladies saw my adventure, didn't you?"

Elizabeth Butler replied, "Yes, we were watching you," she said with a smile. "Only a true animal lover could show such amazing love to an unfamiliar dog."

"Thank you, Elizabeth!" exclaimed Miranda. "I do have a soft spot in my heart for animals. Do any of you know who this dog might belong to? He isn't wearing a collar."

Several of the women said they had no idea. They thought if anyone cared enough about him, they should have a collar on him, in case he ever got lost. Miranda had to agree with them. "If no one claims him, he will become a brother to Herman, Eddie and Lily," she said. "I think I'll call him DRAKE! That seems to fit him. I can tell he is a pure bred Lab and I imagine he would make an excellent duck hunter. I'm sure Gabe would love to take him hunting and see what he can do. Here I am talking like he is already ours. I guess it doesn't hurt to dream, does it?"

"He would have a wonderful home here with you, Miranda," said Elizabeth. "I hope you get to keep him. Robert and I really appreciate you giving our dogs a home."

"We were more than happy to do that. I have been wanting to get a couple of dogs, so that worked out great. They are enjoying life on our ranch. Isabelle has grown so attached to them. They love her, too! She gets lonely and they have been good for her."

"When your baby gets older, Isabelle won't be lonely any longer. Then with her Mom having a baby soon, she will have two playmates," added Elizabeth.

"Indeed she will," replied Miranda.

The crowd starting leaving and around seven-thirty the last guests left. Miranda and Jennifer were tired. Gabe and Mardi told them to relax and they would clean up outside. So Jennifer went to the den, sat down and propped up her feet. Miranda took baby Taylor upstairs and gave her a bath before putting her to bed for the night. Then she came back downstairs and joined Jennifer in the den. Isabelle was outside with her dad.

"I think your cook-out was a success, Miranda!" exclaimed Jennifer as she yawned.

"Yes, I think so, too. Everyone seemed to have a great time. The children had so much fun with the games, didn't they?"

"They did indeed," responded Jennifer. "I think Ethel and Emily outdid themselves with the food!"

"They surely did! I bet this will get even more work for them. The food was delicious and they seemed to enjoy cooking so much. They definitely have a talent."

"Don't forget, so do you!" exclaimed Jennifer.

"Thanks, Jen! I'm glad you like my cooking."

"I do and you know you're much better in the kitchen than I am."

"I do love to cook and always have," replied Miranda.

"I think I'll turn in for the night. Suddenly I am very tired," said Jennifer.

"Goodnight, Jen...hope you sleep well."

"Thanks, Miranda and the same to you."

Chapter 17

Monday morning at breakfast Gabe and Mardi discussed the work situation. They were so busy on the ranch and thought it might be time to hire another work hand. They decided to put an ad in the local paper and see if they could find someone who would be right for the job. They had several calls from the ad, but never any that sounded positive. After finding out the work details most of them decided it wasn't for them. Finally, on the third week they received a call from Wade Helstein. He was thirty years old and had some experience of working with cattle. Gabe asked him to come for an interview the following morning at nine o'clock.

At exactly nine o'clock, Wade pulled into the driveway. Gabe and Mardi went outside to meet him. He was a clean cut looking guy wearing wranglers and a t-shirt. His boots were well polished and he made a good first appearance. He walked up to Gabe and extended his hand, "Hello, I'm Wade Helstein."

"Hello Wade and welcome to our ranch. I'm Gabe Colter and this is my brother-in-law, Mardi Carson."

Mardi shook hands with him and said, "Welcome to the ranch, Wade."

After a brief interview Gabe and Mardi decided that Wade would be a good addition to their cowboys.

"You're hired," said Gabe. Can you report to work in the morning?"

"Sure can," Wade replied with a smile. Thank you, guys. I am looking forward to working for you,"

They talked awhile then took him to the bunk house, where he left the few belongings he had brought with him.

"Do you have any family?" asked Gabe.

"No," he replied. "My parents are dead and I'm an only child. I'm not married either."

"I'm sorry to hear about your parents. They must have been young?"

"They were killed in a car accident."

"Well, welcome to our family," added Gabe with a smile.

"Thank you!" exclaimed Wade.

"We'll leave you to get settled in. Lunch will be served at noon. Hope you have a good appetite. After lunch you can go out with the other guys. They're doing some branding today."

"Sounds good," replied Wade.

Gabe and Mardi turned and left the bunk house. "What do you think of Wade?" asked Gabe.

"He seems like a nice enough guy. Of course, it's a little early to tell what he's like," replied Mardi. "I just hope he will be trustworthy."

"Me, too!" exclaimed Gabe.

The next morning Gabe and Mardi went to the bunk house as the men were finishing breakfast. "Good Morning," said Gabe with a cheerful smile.

"Good Morning, Gabe," the men said in unison.

"Rex, I would like to have a word with you," said Gabe.

"Sure boss," Rex responded. Rex had been the foreman

on the Parker Ranch for many years. As he aged and became unable to do much work, Grayson had given the job to Gabe. Rex still hung out with the cowboys some even though he wasn't able to do much. He was past eighty but seemed to be in good shape for his age. He often gave them advice which they accepted most of the time. This was to be Rex's home as long as he lived. He had nowhere else to go. He loved living here. Since he had never married, this was his family. They all loved him.

After all the guys had left the bunk house, Rex remained behind. "You wanted to see me Mr. Gabe?" he asked.

"Yes, Sir," replied Gabe. "I want to know your opinion on the new guy, Wade."

"I observed him yesterday at lunch and dinner. He was very quiet and didn't have much to say. He seemed to want to keep to himself. That's about all I can tell you, Mr. Gabe. I will keep my eye on him and report any unusual behavior."

"Thank you, Rex," said Gabe. "I knew I could count on you!"

"You know I will always be loyal to you, Mr. Gabe," said Rex with a laugh.

"I know you will and I appreciate you very much!"

Things went well for the next several months. Wade seemed to be working out well. He was a hard worker, but still liked to keep to himself as much as possible. The other guys thought that was a little strange but realized that he was just probably different from them. He was pulling his work load so that was what was most important.

One Thursday evening after dinner he left without saying a word to anyone. He took his few belongings with him. The other guys thought that was strange but never questioned him. They assumed he was taking some time off and would return in a few days. One of them named, Shayne, did go to the main house to ask Gabe about it.

"He never said a word to me," said a surprised Gabe. "I wonder where he could be going and if he will come back to work. I must say I am surprised that he left without saying a word to me."

"Me, too," added Shayne. "I thought he would tell you that he was leaving or at least ask for some time off. That's what the rest of us would do. But then, he seemed different from the rest of us. He was a very private guy and kept to himself most of the time."

"Well, time will tell," said Gabe.

Friday morning came and everything seemed normal. Wade had not come home last night. Gabe noticed he wasn't there but never mentioned it to the other guys. No one brought up the subject even though Gabe was sure they were all wondering about him. Gabe discussed the work details for the day and the guys left to do their duties. He and Mardi got busy with their plans for the day.

Jennifer left for work and Isabelle caught the bus to go to school. Miranda got Taylor ready and headed off to the clinic. Ellie, the nanny, arrived a few minutes after them. She was in a good mood and was excited to see Taylor. She acted so proud of the baby. In fact, she loved her like her own.

Miranda had a very busy morning and never had a chance to slip off to see her beautiful daughter, who was eleven months old now. Around noon she decided to leave the office for a few minutes and go to the nursery. She opened the door expecting to see her baby who would be so excited to see her mommy. To her surprise, the room was empty. Where could they be? Ellie hadn't told her they were going anywhere. Maybe she had taken Taylor out for a walk. But NO...she wouldn't do that without informing me, thought Miranda. Panic was about to set in... She went to the door and looked out. Ellie's car was gone. Now she was really beginning to get stressed... WHERE IS MY BABY???

She ran to the phone as fast as her feet would carry her. She dialed Mardi's cell phone. There was no answer. She dialed again and still no answer. She left him a message telling him to call her. She dialed Gabe's number and got no answer. She also left him a message. She knew they were busy and couldn't answer the phone or didn't even hear it ring.. Her next thought was Jennifer. She quickly dialed her cell phone and Jennifer answered on the third ring. "JENNIFER!!!" she screamed.

"Calm down, Miranda and tell me what's wrong."

"IT'S MY BABY!!!" she screamed. "SHE'S GONE!!!"

"What so you mean, she's gone?" asked Jennifer in a panic. "What's wrong with her?"

"ELLIE'S GONE AND SHE TOOK MY BABY!" she screamed again.

"Maybe she took Taylor outside to play," suggested Jennifer trying to reassure her sister.

"NO, YOU DON'T UNDERSTAND! ELLIE'S CAR IS GONE!!!" she screamed. She was crying so hard and it was very hard for Jennifer to make sense out of what she was saying.

"Maybe they went to get something to eat."

"NO, SHE WOULDN'T DO THAT WITHOUT ASKING ME! JENNIFER, I KNOW SOMETHING IS WRONG! I HAVE A BAD FEELING..." added Miranda still crying very hard.

"Give her a couple more hours and if she isn't back by then, call me back," said Jennifer. "I think you're worrying needlessly."

"I sure hope you're right, but I have a bad feeling about this."

Just as Miranda hung up, her cell phone rang. She saw it was Mardi. "MARDI," she screamed, "I think something has happened to Taylor. SHE'S MISSING!!!"

"MISSING?" asked Mardi in a panic. "What are you talking about?"

"ELLIE HAS TAKEN HER AND THAT'S ALL I KNOW!!!"

"Don't worry, Miranda. Ellie takes good care of Taylor and she'll bring her back. Perhaps she took her out for a stroll. After all, it is a beautiful day." He could hear the panic in Miranda's voice, so he was trying to calm her down.

"What I'm trying to tell you, Mardi, is that Ellie's car is GONE!!!" she exclaimed. "She has never taken her without asking me. Mardi, I just know something is not right!"

"Give her another hour or so and I bet she will bring Taylor back home."

"Mardi, I don't think they'll be back. I am going to call the police. I am not waiting any longer."

"Wait until I get to the house...please, Miranda..."

"Okay, but HURRY!!!" she screamed.

"I'll be right there," he said as he hung up his phone.

Mardi got to the house a few minutes later and could see that Miranda was devastated. He picked up the phone and dialed 911. The dispatcher answered promptly. After hearing what Mardi had to say, he instructed him to wait a couple more hours and if the baby and her nanny hadn't returned, to please call him back.

Miranda was not happy with this. "Time is wasting... Ellie could be leaving town with our baby!!!" she exclaimed through tears.

"Don't be silly," said Mardi. "Ellie would never do something like this."

"I'm not so sure. She sure is attached to Taylor. Too much, if you ask me."

"She's the perfect nanny, Miranda. She would never harm Taylor," added Mardi. "We'll wait two hours and I'm sure they will be back safe and sound."

"I hope you're right," replied Miranda. "I sure hope you're right! What are we going to do for the next two hours? I can't go back to work."

"Neither can I," replied Mardi. "I think we need to pray!"

"Yes, you're right," added Miranda. The two of them knelt down side by side and Mardi led the prayer. He poured his heart out to God and asked for protection for their baby daughter. After he finished, Miranda prayed also. They ended with "In Jesus name, Amen."

Meanwhile, Mardi called all the neighbors surrounding their ranch and asked if anyone had seen a burgundy 2008 Dodge van go by their house. No one had seen a vehicle fitting that description. That's not good, thought Mardi. Surely someone would have seen it.

The next two hours were the longest time of their life. Ellie did not return with their baby. Miranda was getting hysterical by now. "I TOLD YOU SHE HAS TAKEN OUR BABY!!!" she screamed at Mardi.

"You may be right," he said trying to remain calm. "I think it's time to call the police." He dialed 911 again and gave the dispatcher all the info he could think of. He was asking Miranda for info on the clothes both Ellie and the baby were wearing. As she told him, he relayed this on to the dispatcher.

"I'll pass this on to the sheriff and he will put out an APB on them. Hopefully they haven't gotten too far by now. We'll call you as soon as we have some news. Meanwhile, if you hear anything please give us a call."

"We sure will," replied Mardi. "Thank you very much!"

"We're just doing our job," replied the dispatcher as he hung up.

Half an hour later, the phone rang. Mardi let it ring three times before answering it. "Mardi Carson speaking," he said.

"Mr. Carson," said a muffled man's voice. "We have your baby. If you ever want to see her alive, here is what you need to do. DON'T CALL THE POLICE!!! I will get back with you and give you instructions on what to do." The man hung up the phone.

Mardi stood there in a daze holding the phone.

"WHAT'S THE MATTER? WHO WAS THAT?" asked an irate Miranda.

"It's the kidnapper," said Mardi in a shocked voice. "He told me not to call the police. I never told him I already had. I need to call them and let them know what's going on."

The police questioned Mardi about the phone call. Since the man had used the word 'we' that meant he was not acting alone. "Perhaps your nanny and this man conspired together to kidnap your baby. Was your nanny dating anyone?"

"If she was, she never told us," replied Mardi. "In fact, she never talked about her past or her present. She seemed to keep things to herself. WAIT ONE MINUTE...I just had a thought... A few months ago we hired a new cow hand. His name was Wade Helstein. He was a loner and never talked about his past. He never told the guys anything about his life at all. He left here yesterday after dinner and never returned last night or today. This has me thinking... I am wondering if he was somehow connected to our nanny."

"This is a good theory, Mr. Carson. It's something for us to keep in mind. What kind of car did he drive? What did she drive?"

"He had a black 2007 Ford F100 pickup truck. She drove a burgundy 2008 Dodge van.

"So we should be looking for both these vehicles, especially the van. If you hear from them again, call me ASAP. I'm going to send a man out to tap your phones and set up a recording device. When the kidnapper calls back, try to keep him on the line as long as possible so we can trace the call. This will give us an idea where they are"

"I will do that."

Two plain clothed policemen came out twenty minutes later and got all the equipment set up. They stayed nearby and waited.

An hour later another call came in. "Mr. Carson, I want you to listen carefully. If you want to see your baby alive, you need to get us $500,000. I'll give you three days and I'll call back." He hung up the phone too quickly. The police were unable to trace the call.

Mardi had turned as white as a ghost. "He's asking for $500,000. Where am I going to get that kind of money?"

Miranda came over to Mardi and put her arms around him, "We'll find it somewhere, Mardi!" she exclaimed as the tears poured down her face. "We'll borrow on the clinic... I'm sure Gabe and Jennifer will help us also."

"I'm sure you're right, Miranda. I can't go to the bank until Monday. We'll talk to Gabe and Jennifer tonight."

"We'll stay on top of this," added the policeman named Dan.

His partner, Ryker, said, "You can count on us."

"Thank you, guys!" exclaimed Mardi. "We really appreciate your help and concern. We have to get our baby back, no matter what."

"Don't worry," said Ryker. "We'll get her back for you."

"Thank you!" exclaimed Mardi as he stood there holding a tearful Miranda.

Saturday and Sunday were the longest days ever. Mardi and Miranda couldn't eat or sleep. They were in constant prayer for their beautiful daughter's safety.

When Monday morning came, they were at the bank in Laurel at nine o'clock. They walked in as soon as the door was opened and asked to see the President of the bank. Mr. Bolton saw them immediately. When he heard their request, he was very sympathetic. "Of course, I will loan you the money. With the clinic and your half of the ranch, you have plenty of collateral. It will be tomorrow before I can have the money," he told them.

"The kidnapper is going to call today. He said Friday that we had until today to come up with the money. Maybe he will wait one more day," sighed Mardi.

"He won't have a choice. I don't have that much money here. I'll have to get it from the home branch office."

"Thank you very much, Mr. Bolton!" exclaimed Mardi as he shook the man's hand. Miranda followed suit and they hurriedly exited the bank.

Back home Mardi thanked Gabe for his offer of help the night before. Mardi had told him to wait and see what the bank could do for them. He felt relieved that Mr. Bolton came through for them. If only the kidnapper could wait one more day. He prayed and asked God to take care of this matter. He knew God would not let him down.

At five o'clock the phone rang. The police were ready

with their tracing equipment. Mardi picked up the phone and said hello. After a brief hesitation, a male voice spoke clearly.

"Do you have the money?" he asked.

"I won't have it until tomorrow," said Mardi. The perspiration was pouring down his face. "We went to the bank this morning, but the president didn't have that much money locally. He has to get it from the home office."

"I TOLD YOU TODAY," the man shouted. "My patience is running short!"

"I'm doing the best I can. Please give me one more day and don't hurt my baby," he pleaded.

"I guess I can wait another day. You had better have the money by noon tomorrow, or you will never see your baby again."

"PLEASE," pleaded Mardi. "I will have the money by then. I'll be at the bank when it opens in the morning."

"I will call you at noon and tell you where to drop off the money."

"I need for you to bring my baby and we'll make the exchange," said Mardi.

"Listen, Mr. Hot Shot...I'm the one calling the shots now. You'll do exactly what I say or else! I am reminding you again...no cops!"

"I hear you," said Mardi with tears in his eyes. "I will come alone."

Chapter 18

The night seemed to drag by. Miranda and Mardi never slept a wink. Both of them were getting very tired. They had not slept since little Taylor was kidnapped.

Tuesday morning came and that found them once again at the bank at nine o'clock. Mr. Bolton had the money waiting for them. With attaché case in hand, they walked out of the bank carrying $500,000. Neither of them were worried about the money...they just wanted their daughter back safe and sound.

Mardi drove back to the ranch and they waited. It was two hours until the meeting time. Mardi thought of nothing else. He hoped and prayed this all carried out like the FBI had planned. The local police thought it would be wise to involve the FBI in the case. They were much more trained for situations like this. Each agent had been instructed of their position near the site. The meeting place would be surrounded with agents.

Mardi left the house at eleven thirty. He drove slowly to the meeting place in the country. He had no way of knowing where the agents were hiding, but felt secure they were already in place. Even knowing this, he was still nervous. "Please, Dear God," he prayed out loud, "Please let everything go as planned and bring our baby home safely to us. I give you all the honor and praise. In Jesus name I pray. Amen!" Somehow he began to have a feeling of peace come over him. He knew God was able to take care of his baby girl and he was trusting Him to do just that.

He arrived ten minutes early and parked the car. He turned off the motor and waited. At exactly twelve noon, he saw a burgundy van heading from the opposite direction. He immediately recognized the van and knew for certain that Wade Helstein and Ellie Livingston were the kidnappers. The van slowed down to a stop and the man turned off the motor. He got out of his vehicle and headed toward Mardi who had just gotten out of his vehicle carrying the attaché case.

"Do you have the money?" yelled Wade.

"I have the money, but I want my daughter!" exclaimed Mardi.

"You'll get your daughter, but I want the money first. I want to make sure you are not pulling a fast one on me."

Mardi opened the attaché case and showed Wade the money, then instantly closed it. "Tell Ellie to bring the baby to me. I know she's in this with you."

"I am the one in control, Mr. Big Shot. You just remember that!" he screamed. "I want that money, NOW!"

"I want my baby!" yelled Mardi. "This is supposed to be an exchange!"

"GIVE ME THE MONEY or you will not see your baby alive!" Wade yelled.

Wade was not cooperating like they had hoped. From out of nowhere, the special agents swarmed around him as he drew his gun. Not waiting for him to fire, several of the agents fired at the same time. Wade dropped to ground with four bullets holes in his chest and head. He died instantly. The other agents rushed to the van where Ellie and the baby were. They took her in custody for being an accessory to the crime of kidnapping. They took the baby to her Daddy, who by now was crying tears of joy.

"Oh, baby Taylor, I was so afraid I wouldn't see you again," he said to her as he held her closely and let the tears fall. "Let's go home to Mommy." They turned and headed to the truck. When he pulled into the driveway, Miranda was out the door like a flash.

"Oh, my baby...," cried Miranda as she ran to the truck. She instantly took Taylor into her arms and gave her a tight squeeze. "Thank you, Mardi," she cried as she looked at her husband. "Thank you for rescuing our baby! I'm never going to let her out of my sight again!"

"God was good to us! He took care of our precious baby and brought her home to us safely!"

"I know," said a tearful Miranda. "I am so thankful for all of God's blessings."

Gabe, Jennifer and Isabelle were waiting for them at the door. They were all smiles as Mardi and Miranda walked up the steps with their daughter.

"Welcome home," said Jennifer. "Mardi, we were praying for you and asked God to handle the situation."

"Thank you!" exclaimed Mardi. "I do give God the credit but He used the FBI agents to carry out the return of our daughter. Had they not been there, I shudder to think of what might have happened. Wade was a determined man. When the policemen saw he wasn't cooperating, they moved in and took him down. It was not a pretty sight but they did the only thing left to do. I thought I knew Wade but I saw a completely different side of him today."

"Was Ellie in on it, too?" asked Gabe.

"Yes, she was. None of us ever realized they were connected. It sure shocked me. Now she will be spending a long time in jail. I have a feeling that they had this all planned before they both got a job on the ranch. They picked out a family with doctors and figured it would be an easy target. I'm sure it seemed simple to them but when God takes over, He works it all out for the good of those who love Him. Both of them seemed so nice... I am just so sorry they turned out bad!"

"Me, too!" exclaimed Gabe. "Both of them seemed so good at their job. Maybe they were trying extra hard so we would learn to trust them."

"I know one thing," assured Miranda. "I will be more careful when I look for another nanny."

"We will have the next one thoroughly checked out!"

"I thought we did with Ellie. She sure had a perfect résumé!"

"I know. Don't blame yourself, Miranda. It could have happened to anyone. We just happened to be their target."

"I am going to hire someone I know next time. I was thinking...about Ethel's and Emily's older sister, Sallie. She is about sixty but I think she would make a wonderful nanny. This might be the very thing she needs to bring her out of the depression she suffers with. I think I will call her and see if she is interested."

"I like your way of thinking, my dear!" exclaimed Mardi with a smile.

"I will call her first thing in the morning. I need the rest of the day to get my nerves settled. It has been a terrible few days."

"Indeed, it has. I am so glad we have God on our side. I wouldn't want to go one day without Him."

"Me, neither!" Miranda exclaimed. "I am going to take Taylor upstairs and give her a bath. She seems more tired than usual. I hope she sleeps well tonight."

"She should since she'll be back in her own bed. Goodnight, baby girl," he said as he kissed her. "I'm sure we'll all sleep better tonight."

Chapter 19

She gave Sallie a call around nine o'clock the next morning. Sallie was excited to hear from Miranda whom she had known for many years. Rachel used to bring the children to visit her sometimes. She really missed those days!

"Sallie, I guess you wonder why I'm calling so early this morning."

"Yes, I do. Is something wrong?"

"Yes and no...Did you hear about our baby being kidnapped last Friday?" asked Miranda.

"I did hear a little about it and I was praying for all of you."

"Thank you, Sallie. I guess you know my babysitter was involved with the kidnapping."

"I did hear that," she replied. "I am so sorry. What are you going to do for a babysitter?"

"That's why I'm calling you this morning. Would be possibly be interested in taking care of Taylor while I work? The nursery is in my clinic and I'm only a few doors away."

"You know...I think I might be interested. That would get me away from the house during the day. Ethel and Emily worry about me a lot. This would help ease their mind I'm sure."

"Great!" exclaimed Miranda. "Can you start in the morning?"

"I sure can. I don't have anything to keep me from starting right away," added Sallie. She sounded more upbeat than she did when Miranda first called her. Miranda knew this might be the answer to Sallie's happiness. It sure would be an answer to prayer for Miranda and Mardi.

"Thank you, Sallie!" exclaimed Miranda. "I'll be looking for you around nine in the morning."

"I'll be there, Lord willing. Goodbye!"

"Goodbye, Sallie."

Miranda gave Mardi a quick call and let him know the arrangements she had made with Sallie. He was very happy, too. Now they wouldn't have to worry about their baby girl. She was taking the day off since she didn't have a babysitter so she and Taylor would have a Mother/Daughter day although Taylor was too small to know anything about such things.

The next morning Sallie arrived a few minutes before nine o'clock. She had a smile on her face and seemed in a good spirit. This pleased Miranda. She felt this was going to work out fine. "Good morning, Sallie. Nice to see you again and thank you so much for accepting this position."

"I feel honored that you trust me to take care of your precious baby," said Sallie with a smile on her face. She actually felt happy today for the first time in a long time. Maybe this was just the thing she needed, she thought to herself. She was grateful that Miranda gave her this chance.

"Thank you!" exclaimed Miranda. "Now, come meet Taylor Lynn." They walked down the hallway to the nursery where Taylor was sleeping. Sallie settled in the easy chair and looked lovingly at the baby in her care. "I have a shelf of books you might like to read while Taylor is sleeping. Take your pick."

"Thank you! I love to read! I have done a lot of reading since my husband left me. It helps pass the time."

"I'm so sorry for what you've been through. It's his loss...he doesn't know what he gave up."

"I tried to tell him that before he left," said Sallie with a half smile.

"Make yourself comfortable. Read, watch TV or eat," laughed Miranda. "There's a mini fridge and microwave over there," she said pointing to them. "Help yourself to anything you want to eat or drink. I'll bring your lunch to you each day."

"Why, thank you! I can't ask for anything better than this!" Sallie exclaimed with a big smile.

"I am just so happy to have you here taking care of Taylor. It means so much to know I can trust you and not worry about my baby."

"I'll take the best care of her that I can."

"I know you will, Sallie. Thank you again!"

"You're welcome. I think this will be good for all of us."

"I'll see you at lunch time."

She had an extra busy day since she was closed yesterday. Business was going really well for her and she was very thankful for that. She had so many things to be thankful for. God had taken care of their little angel and brought her back safely to them. That was the one thing she was most thankful for.

Week after week went by. Taylor was growing and Sallie was doing a great job with her. This was the best thing that could have happened for both of them. Taylor was growing more attached to Sallie every day. Sallie thought there was no one like Taylor. This was the baby she never had. She was so thankful for the opportunity to work for this loving family.

****

Jennifer's pregnancy was progressing. She was doing well except for feeling tired. She worked long days at the clinic and decided she must cut her hours until after the baby came. She decided to work six hours a day for the rest of her pregnancy. This seemed to be much easier for her. Gabe was really glad since he had been the one to first suggest it. He was very concerned about Jennifer and their baby. She had just found out they were having another girl. Isabelle was thrilled. Both Jennifer and Gabe were happy, too. Jennifer thought Gabe probably would have liked to have a boy, but he never showed any disappointment when they were told it was a girl.

"Gabe," said Jennifer as she was getting ready for bed one night. "I have been thinking about a name for our baby. I would like to name her Rachel Rose. What do you think?"

"Rachel Rose," he pondered this in his mind for a minute and replied, "I think Rachel Rose is a beautiful name. That would be after you and your mother. I'm sure Rachel would be happy."

"She would be..." sighed Jennifer. "I would like for her name to be carried on. Can you understand this, Gabe?"

"Sure I can. Rachel was the strength of this family and I think it's only appropriate that she should be honored."

"Good!" exclaimed Jennifer with a big smile. She went over to Gabe and put her arms around him and gave him a tender kiss. "You're the best husband ever, Gabe Colter!"

"Thank you," said Gabe with a smile. "I'll accept that," he teased.

Chapter 20

Things had returned to normal on the Parker Ranch. Sallie was working out very well as a nanny for Taylor. She thought the sun rose and set in Taylor. Meanwhile, Taylor was becoming very much attached to her also. Miranda was very happy to see them bonding so well. Sallie had become a part of their family. Miranda and Mardi were so thankful for her.

They were all sitting at the dinner table one evening when the phone rang. Jennifer got up and said, "I'll get it." She answered the phone and was in complete shock. They rest of the family could tell from her voice that something 'big' was going on.

"When Caycee?" she asked. "Of course you may. Call me back with the details and we'll get everything set up. Goodbye."

"What was that all about?" asked Miranda as Jennifer sat back down at the table with a stunned look on her face.

"My dear sister that was Caycee calling from California. It seems that she and Harley stayed in touch while she was in Paris. After her fashion show was finished she headed straight to California. Now they are planning to get married."

"GET MARRIED?" asked a stunned Miranda. "When's all this going to take place?"

"Hold on to your seats...Caycee wants to have the wedding here on the ranch!"

"Really?" asked Gabe and Mardi in unison.

"Really!" exclaimed Jennifer.

"Oh, that is exciting!" exclaimed Miranda. "That is exactly what this ranch needs! That will give me a chance to show my expertise in cooking, that is, if she wants me to."

"She is going to call back with more details. I told her we would be glad to help out. I think she wants us to do the food. We should ask Ethel and Emily to help out. It will be too much on you, Miranda. With your job and the baby, and of course, Mardi...you have your hands full," said Jennifer with a smile. "We'll all do whatever we can to help them."

"Of course, we will," added Miranda with a smile. "I am so happy for her and Harley."

"I just hope she is the right choice for Harley. He is such a good guy!" exclaimed Jennifer.

"She changed after she became a Christian. We'll just have to pray that she continues to walk with the Lord. If she does everything should be fine with this marriage."

"We'll give her a chance," said Gabe. "That's all we can do, except pray."

"That's what I intend to do," replied Jennifer. "Caycee and Harley are so different and only the Lord can keep them together. I just don't want to see him get hurt!"

"What about her?" asked Gabe.

"I don't worry about Harley hurting her. He will make a very devoted husband. I just hope she will be worthy of him."

"Sounds like you know him pretty well!" exclaimed Gabe.

"I do, but only as a good friend," she replied. "If

I didn't know better, Gabe Colter, I'd think you were jealous."

"I am not jealous," he replied with a grin. "I was just curious to see how well you know Harley."

"You can set your mind at ease, Gabe; we were never more than friends!"

"Okay, I'm glad to know that."

"I have been yours from the first day we met even if I did marry another man before I married you. I would never have done that if you hadn't gotten married first."

"I should never have gotten married but I thought I had lost you forever!" Gabe exclaimed.

"Even though it took us a few years to get together, it was in God's plan all along."

"Of course, it was!" exclaimed Gabe. He leaned over and gave Jennifer a hug and added, "I thank God for you every day and will never take you for granted, my love!"

"I feel the same way, Gabe," she said as she leaned over and kissed him.

"You're not supposed to be kissing at the dinner table," said a laughing little Isabelle.

"We're sorry, Isy!" exclaimed Jennifer. "This was a special occasion which called for a kiss."

"Ooooh...okay," Isabelle chuckled. "We'll let you by with it this time."

Everyone was laughing along with Isabelle. They continued to finish their dinner while the conversation was mostly about Caycee's and Harley's wedding. They were all excited about it. They were happy that Caycee wanted to get married at the ranch. They were glad that she felt close enough to them to want to have the wedding here. This gave them all something exciting to look forward to. Heaven knows they needed it, after all the trials they had faced over the past years.

Chapter 21

Miranda's practice was doing well. She was even considering hiring another doctor to help out. In fact her business was doing so well that it was almost more than she and her nurse Sandra could do. It briefly ran through her mind to ask Dr. Laura Fisher but she knew Laura would never leave Prince Edward Island. Her husband, Shan, was from there also and that's where their family lived. It was just a happy thought for a fleeting moment. She would give it a little more thought and probably would advertise in the Billings newspaper.

She had just gone out front to check with the receptionist, Debbie, when in walked a girl carrying a beautiful Siberian Husky puppy. Miranda gasped her breath. This was the first one she had seen since she left her dogs on Prince Edward Island with her brother, Rob and his wife, Kati. She missed her Husky dogs!

"What a beautiful puppy!!!" exclaimed Miranda. "How old is he?"

"Thank you, Dr. Sterling. He is 9 weeks old. I'm afraid I'm not going to be able to keep him. I am moving into an apartment and no pets are allowed. I brought Nukilik here today to see if you could find a good home for him."

"Oh, that is too bad, Miss..."

"Kane... Christi Kane," replied the young girl who looked to be in her early twenties.

"I know I can find a home for him, Christi. In fact I would love to have him myself. I am a Husky lover. I had six of them before I moved back to the ranch."

"SIX?" Christi asked in amazement. "What happened to them?"

"I used to live on Prince Edward Island and that is a long way from here. My brother and his wife live there, too. So when I decided to move back to the ranch, they were willing to keep my dogs. I must say I miss them a lot. What did you say your dog's name is again?"

"Nukilik, which mean 'strong' and I call him Nuk."

"I like that name. Nukilik he will remain. Has he had any of his shots?"

"Only the first ones," replied Christi. "I have his vet record with me. I also have all of his papers. I bought him from 'HOWL'N WIND' in Van Dyne, Wisconsin."

"Oh, really?" asked Miranda smiling. That's where some of my dogs came from. I am very familiar with that place. They have wonderful dogs!"

Christi handed the folder to Miranda, who laid it on the desk. "Debbie, will you file this in my 'Personal' file for now?"

"Sure, Dr. Sterling," said Debbie as she took the folder to the file cabinet and placed it in the proper drawer.

Christi handed her dog to Miranda with a sad look on her face. Miranda could tell she really loved the dog and could feel her sorrow at having to give him up. "Wait just a minute, Christi. Let me put Nukilik in a crate and I will be back shortly."

"Okay, Dr. Sterling."

Miranda took Nukilik and placed him in a crate inside her personal office. He needed to be around her and not shut off from human contact. It would take him awhile to get used to his new owner. She picked up her purse and took out her check book. She wrote a check to Christi for $500. She knew how expensive Huskies were and thought this might help ease Christi's pain of having to give him up. She went back to the front desk where Christi was waiting. She handed the check to her and said, "Maybe this will help you, Christi. I know how hard it is to give up your beloved pet."

Christi took one look at the check and let out a gasp. "Oh Dr. Sterling, I wasn't asking money for my dog. I just wanted to find him a good home."

"I know Christi. I also know how expensive these dogs are so I wanted to help ease your pain."

Christi walked over to Miranda and put her arms around her neck. "Oh Dr. Sterling, you don't know what this means to me. I thank you from the bottom of my heart!"

"You are very welcome, Christi. Thank you for bringing Nukilik to my office. I am so happy to have another Husky dog. You can come visit him anytime you want to."

"Thank you, Dr. Sterling!" exclaimed Christi as her eyes lit up. "I may just do that sometime!"

"My door is always open to you, Christi."

"Thank you!" she said as she walked out the door, got into her car and left.

"Well, well, Debbie, I finally have a Husky dog," said Miranda with a big smile. "This has truly made my day. I'm not sure what Mardi will say since we already have four dogs."

"Oh, he won't care," replied Debbie. "He just wants you to be happy!"

"You are right, Debbie. I have the best husband in the world!"

Later that afternoon when it was time to close the office, she put a leash on Nukilik and led him out of the office. He was excited to be outside. He tried to run and it was all Miranda could do to keep up with him. He was very strong for such a young puppy.

Sallie offered to bring Taylor to the house since Miranda had the puppy. They left at the same time. Taylor was watching Nukilik as if to say, "What is he doing here?" She was giggling like any little girl would. Miranda felt joy in her heart just watching her baby girl. She could see the happiness on Sallie's face as she carried Taylor. They had really bonded.

Jennifer was already home from work when Miranda and Sallie arrived. She could not believe her eyes when she saw Miranda had another dog. She knew Miranda had always been a sucker for every stray animal ever since she had been a little girl.

"So who do we have here?" asked Jennifer in surprise.

"Meet Nukilik, Jennifer!" she exclaimed as she brought him into the house.

"What are you doing with him?" asked Jennifer.

"He's mine...he will be joining our family. Taylor already likes him!"

"I can see that! Has Mardi seen him yet?"

"Not yet," replied Miranda.

About that time Mardi and Gabe came in the back door. Nukilik ran over to greet them and started licking Mardi's hand. "Well, well...who are you?" he asked looking straight at Miranda.

"Oh, Mardi and Gabe, I'd like for you to meet Nukilik. He is the newest addition to our family."

"Hello, Nukilik," said Mardi and Gabe in unison.

"What do you think, Mardi?" asked Miranda with a smile.

"I think he's beautiful and if he's yours, I say welcome," he replied.

"Oh, thank you, Mardi! A girl named Christi brought him to the clinic. She had to find a home for him and wanted me to help her."

"So you helped her, didn't you?" he asked teasingly.

"I sure did! I was ready and willing!" she exclaimed with a laugh.

"Oh, well...what's one more, right?" asked Gabe with a grin. "It's a good thing we have a big ranch for them to run on."

"Yes, I am thankful we have this wonderful ranch. It is a great place for animals as well as us," stated Miranda.

Jennifer had been watching and listening. "We are all so blessed to have this wonderful place to live and to have each other. We must never take any of it for granted. Life is so short; it's like a vapor. We are only here for a season, and then we will join our Heavenly Father in Heaven. That is the only important thing in life...is to be ready to go meet our Savior when He calls for us. We know not what day or hour He will call us home. We will leave all these earthly possessions behind. This is nothing compared to what He has in store for us!"

"Well spoken my dear sister!" exclaimed Miranda. "It makes me 'Homesick for Heaven' sometimes when I really dwell on it."

"I know the feeling," responded Jennifer.

Chapter 22

The next few months went by quickly. Jennifer was not feeling so well lately. It was getting close to time for her delivery. She and Gabe were very excited to be having another baby. They just prayed for a normal, healthy baby girl. They had definitely decided her name would be Rachel Rose Colter. This gave Jennifer peace of mind knowing that memories of her mom would live on in their new baby daughter.

Two weeks later Jennifer went into labor at work. She wasn't due for three more weeks, so this came as a shock to her. She was having hard pains in her stomach and back. She knew what she had to do, so she called Gabe's cell phone. There was no answer and she left a message. Meanwhile she called the house and talked to Miranda, who told her that Gabe was out on the range.

"I will try to find him, Jennifer. Don't worry he will be there as soon as possible. Good luck and God be with you and your baby. I love you. Now get yourself over to the hospital and have us a baby," said Miranda with delight.

"I'm on my way and thank you, Sis. I love you, too!"

Jennifer walked across to the hospital, which seemed like the longest walk of her life. Her pains were getting closer and more intense. "Please God," she prayed, "Let me make it to the ER in time." As soon as she arrived they wheeled her into the delivery room. Gabe wasn't there when she gave birth to their seven pound baby girl. She was back in a room on the OB ward when Gabe came strolling in.

"I am sooo sorry I didn't make it in time, Jennifer," he said with all sincerity as he leaned down and kissed her. "I came just as quickly as I could. I broke the speed limit, but fortunately there were no policemen around," he said with a nervous laugh. "Now, where is our daughter?"

At that moment, a nurse walked into the room carrying a little bundle wrapped in a pink blanket. "Mr. Colter would you like to hold your baby daughter?" she asked.

"Sure I would," he replied as he took the baby into his arms. He leaned over and kissed her on the forehead. "Rachel Rose, you are one beautiful baby girl! You are more beautiful than the fairest of all the roses!"

"Now, isn't she? I think she looks like her daddy."

"Look at that long blonde hair! She takes that after her grandmother, Rachel. Look at her rosy cheeks! Rose is the perfect name for her. I'm glad we have named her 'Rachel Rose' after you and your Mother."

"I like that," responded Jennifer. "She is our little Rose sent from Heaven! God has been so good to us in giving us another beautiful baby girl."

"Indeed He has!" exclaimed Gabe. "We will dedicate her to the Lord."

"Absolutely! Now, Gabe, we need to call the family and tell them the wonderful news."

"Of course, my dear!" He handed the baby to Jennifer and took out his cell phone. He called his parents and siblings first. Then he called Miranda, Jordan, Rob and Blake. Everyone was so excited and congratulated them. The next day flowers arrived from many of them, along with gifts for the baby.

Jennifer and little Rachel Rose came home a couple days later. Jennifer seemed very quiet as if she was in a deep thought.

"Is something wrong?" asked Gabe as he gave her a hug.

"No, I just feel a little sad that Mom and Dad aren't here to see their new granddaughter," she answered. "I wish Aunt Pat and Uncle Roman were here, too! I miss all of them so very much."

"I know you do my love and I miss them also," stated Gabe. "You know Aunt Pat and Uncle Roman lived a long time. God allowed us to keep them until they were old and feeble. He saw fit to take them HOME when they weren't able to take care of themselves any longer. After Aunt Pat died, Uncle Roman lost the will to live and followed her just three weeks later. They're together now, just like your Mom and Dad. I know they're all happy in their Heavenly Home."

"I know they are, too, but I still miss them!" she exclaimed. "Things will never be the same anymore."

"Life has to go on, my love! We weren't born to live forever. We had an appointed time to be born and also have an appointed time to die. We are the parents now and one day our children will be the next generation to carry on. That's how it goes."

"I know," she sighed. About that time a neighbor pulled into the driveway. Isabelle jumped out of the car and ran inside.

"Hi Mom," she yelled. "Where's my baby sister?"

"In here," replied Jennifer.

Isabelle came bounding into the room with much excitement showing in her face. She took one look at the baby and asked excitely, "Can I hold her?"

"May I hold her?" corrected her Mom.

"Oh well, MAY I hold her?" she asked with a frown on her face.

"Yes, you may," added Jennifer with a smile. "Come sit beside me."

Isabelle sat down beside her mom and Jennifer handed the baby to her. The frown left and the look on Isabelle's face was priceless. You would have thought she was the mom. "Oh, Mom...she is so beautiful!" she exclaimed.

"Yes, she is," replied Jennifer. "I think she looks a lot like you."

"Really?" asked Isabelle with a big grin on her face. "Was I this pretty?"

"Of course you were, my dear," Gabe decided to add his thoughts. "We now have two beautiful daughters!"

"I'm glad I have a baby sister," Isabelle added with a grin.

"Me, too," replied Gabe. "Along with little Taylor, we will have three beautiful little girls growing up on the ranch. A whole new generation."

Chapter 23

Later that evening there was a call from Caycee. She was all excited about her upcoming wedding to Harley. She had been making arrangements and had everything in place except for the final details on the ranch. The wedding was only two months away. Jennifer was glad that she had a couple months to recuperate before the big event. Knowing Caycee, it would be a really BIG event!

"Guess what, Jennifer?" she asked.

"What?" Jennifer had no idea what was on Caycee's mind.

"I designed my own wedding gown!" she exclaimed excitedly.

"YOU DID?" She thought Caycee would buy a famous designer gown. But then Caycee was pretty well-known also.

"I did and it's already finished. It was made and shipped to me from Paris. I received it yesterday. I just had to call and tell you!"

"Congratulations, I think that's wonderful! It will be extra special to wear your own creation!"

"I k-n-o-w," added Caycee with excitement in her voice. "I am so excited about the wedding. I know I couldn't find a nicer guy than Harley. He is so good to me and makes me feel like I'm the only woman in the world!"

"That's great, Caycee! I know Harley is a great guy

and I'm so happy that God brought you two together," said Jennifer. "Hold on to God and to each other. For you know...

THE FAMILY, WHO PRAYS TOGETHER, STAYS TOGETHER. I think that is very true."

"I know, Jennifer. I have been so much happier since I became a Christian. Everything doesn't go smoothly all the time but when you know God, things are much easier to deal with."

"Amen to that!" exclaimed Jennifer. "We've had so many things to deal with here on the ranch and if we didn't know the Lord, I don't know how we would have made it through all the tragedy we've had to face."

"I know you've really been through a lot. I pray everything will be good from now on. I need to get off the phone and get some work done. I will be there a week before the wedding so I can get everything lined up."

"Sounds good, Caycee. We look forward to seeing you. Bye for now."

"Goodbye, Jennifer," added Caycee and hung up the phone.

The next two months passed quickly with several phone calls from Caycee wanting advice from Jennifer or Miranda. Jennifer was almost back to normal and baby, Rachel Rose, was doing well. Jennifer planned to go back to work when the baby was three months old. She sure was dreading to leave her. It had been so long since Isabelle and Isac were babies. As much as she loved them she seemed to be enjoying this baby even more. Maybe it was because she was getting older. She also knew this would be their last one. Sometimes she wished she didn't have to go back to work at all, but she knew people needed her and she felt good knowing she could help someone. Besides when she was home and had more free time she let her mind wander to Isac and how he had been taken from them at such a young age of six. She didn't question God... she would never do that, but her heart still yearned for her little son. She knew Isabelle missed him, too. After all he was her twin brother. God had a purpose for Isac and it was comforting to her to know that he was in Heaven. As much as she needed him, God needed him more. He had loaned Isac to them for a short while. She was thankful and knew how blessed they were to have known him for that short time.

Caycee arrived the next day. Jennifer met her at the airport at three o'clock. They had a happy reunion. When all her luggage was loaded, they headed toward the ranch. Caycee was so wound up and never quit talking. Every now and then Jennifer was able to get a word in.

"I can't wait to see your dress!" exclaimed Caycee. "I am so happy you and Miranda are going to be my Bridesmaids!"

"We are happy that you asked us and are looking forward to the wedding very much! Our dresses are beautiful! I love the light shade of lavender. It goes well with Miranda's blonde hair and also my dark hair."

"I know you'll both look beautiful!" exclaimed Caycee with a smile.

"Talking about beautiful, I can't wait to see your wedding gown."

"I am so pleased with it. I hope it won't be too wrinkled. I need to unpack it as soon as we arrive at the ranch."

"That is a good idea. Cayee, I was wondering who you are having for your Maid of Honor."

"Oh, that would be a long time friend from back home. Her name is Jodee Williams. She is a beautiful red head."

"Well, we will all be different, won't we?"

"You will, indeed!' exclaimed Caycee.

"When will she be here?"

"Two days before the wedding. She couldn't come any sooner. She's a prosecuting attorney and had a very important murder case coming up and could not leave. Hopefully they will get it all over. I would be so upset if she didn't make it for the wedding."

"I'm sure you would," replied Jennifer. "We need to pray that God will work it all out so that she can be here on time."

"Let's do that right now." So they joined hands and both said a prayer. Jennifer was driving so she had to pray with her eyes open. She knew God would understand.

They arrived at the ranch and pulled into the driveway. Jennifer helped Caycee get her luggage into the house and upstairs. The house was empty except for them. Miranda was still at work. Isabelle was at the clinic helping Sallie, the nanny, with baby Rachel Rose and little Taylor. She thought she was so big helping with the babies. Sallie said she was such good help and that made Isabelle feel so big and important.

Caycee decided to rest awhile before dinner. First she needed to unpack her wedding gown. Jennifer couldn't wait to see it. When Caycee unfolded it, Jennifer gasped. It was the most beautiful gown she had ever seen in her entire life. Caycee would probably be the most beautiful Bride she had ever seen too, unless it was Miranda.

Jennifer went downstairs and decided to get dinner started. She knew Miranda would help when she came home. It was such a joy to work with her sister. They got along so well. She was so thankful they had each other.

Jennifer was still working when Miranda came in the

door carrying Taylor. Sallie was behind with Rachel Rose in her arms and Isabelle followed her.

"Hello everyone!" exclaimed Jennifer. "Caycee's here! She's upstairs resting."

"I'm glad to know she made it safely," replied Miranda.

"Me, too," said Sallie. "Do you want me to stay awhile and help with the babies?"

"Oh, no..." said Miranda. "You've had your hands full today. You need to go home and rest. Tomorrow's another day..."

"Okay, I'll see you in the morning," said Sallie as she headed for the door.

"Thank you so much for helping with Isabelle and Rachel Rose!"

"It was my pleasure! They are such good children."

"Thanks!" exclaimed Jennifer.

Dinner was on the table when the guys walked in. They went to wash their hands before sitting down at the table. Caycee had woke up and come downstairs without them having to wake her. She entered the kitchen just as everyone was ready to sit down. "Hello, everyone! How are you?" She was very cheerful.

"We're fine," said Gabe as he got up and shook her hand. "Welcome back to the ranch!"

"Thank you, Gabe."

"We're glad to see you again," said Mardi extending his hand. She ignored it and gave him a hug. He was surprised and a little bit embarrassed. He looked directly at Miranda, who was smiling. It didn't seem to bother her now and he was glad. "Are you ready for your big day?" he asked Caycee.

"I think I am," she replied. "I still have some last minute details to see about. Everything seems to be falling into place. Harley, his parents and his two Groomsmen, Mike and Pete, will be here the day before the wedding. Harley's Dad, Sean, is Best Man. He is not well, but wanted so badly to be here for the wedding."

"Well, I sure hope he is able to come," replied Mardi. "Will they need to be picked up at the airport?"

"No, they have rented a car which will be waiting for them. That will make things easier for everyone."

"You know we will be glad to help in any way!" exclaimed Mardi.

"Matter of fact, I do have a request for you, Mardi," chirped Caycee. "I have something I would like for you to do for me."

"What would that be?" asked Mardi rolling his eyes around to see if Miranda was watching. She was… He was almost afraid to ask.

"I would like for you to hitch up some horses and the carriage. After the ceremony, I would like for you to take Harley and me for a ride out along the creek. I would like to go back in time and try to imagine how it was in the Old West days."

"Oh," replied Mardi with relief. "I think that can be arranged."

"Thank you! I will really look forward to that!"

"Consider it done," replied Mardi.

It was good to have Caycee back home. They all joined in the conversation at the dinner table. Everyone seemed to be in such a good mood. This sure pleased Jennifer and Miranda. There was much excitement in the air with the upcoming wedding. The ranch was such a beautiful place for a wedding. Gabe and Mardi would take care of all the outside details. The girls were thankful for their husband's willingness to help.

"Caycee, where are you going on your honeymoon?" asked Miranda.

"We plan to travel several places in the USA. One thing I would like to do while we are here so close, is go see the Glacier National Park. I know that Uncle Grayson worked there and I am interested in knowing more about it. I've done a little research about it and found that the Glacier has pristine forests, alpine meadows, rugged mountains and spectacular lakes. With over seven hundred miles of trails, Glacier is a hiker's paradise. The old days can be relived through historic chalets, lodges, transportation and stories of Native Americans. Weather in the mountains can be fickle. It may be in the 90's with clear and sunny skies and then you may see snow showers and falling temperatures the same day. I can't wait to go there and experience it firsthand. We plan to stay there a few nights and go hiking."

"Sounds like a lot of fun," replied Miranda. "Dad took us there when we were children. It is a fun place to go. Just be careful and don't get lost."

"I'm sure Harley will take good care of me," Caycee said with a laugh.

"Of course, he will!" exclaimed Miranda.

Chapter 24

Rob, Kati and little Grayson arrived from Prince Edward Island a few days before the wedding. Rob was so happy to be back home on the ranch. It had been a few years since he had been home. He was glad to see his sisters again. He was happy to see his brothers, Jordan and Blake also. Even though the guys were not actually related to him, he felt that they were. They all had a happy reunion. Blake was still single and enjoying the Hollywood life. He had many stories to tell them as they sat in the den each night enjoying each other's company.

The DJ had been selected and Caycee had sent him a list of songs she wanted played at the wedding. Brian Heath was good at what he did. He often went to Hollywood to DJ in various affairs. Sometimes he would escort a famous actress to an affair. He was well-known in Hollywood. They were lucky to get him since he stayed so busy.

Multiple kinds of flowers had been ordered in an array of colors. It would be very beautiful. Caycee wanted flowers everywhere! She had wanted an Ice Sculpture, but decided against that due to the warm weather. She had ordered a dozen white doves to be released during the ceremony. She also had butterflies coming. These would be released at the end of the ceremony. She wanted her wedding to be perfect!

They had a very busy week getting everything ready

for the wedding. Gabe and Mardi worked on the outside, while the girls worked inside getting the decorations ready. They didn't have to worry about the food since Ethel and Emily, owners of Et & Em Catering were providing it. Sallie was also coming to care for Taylor Lynn and Rachel Rose. They were too young to enjoy the wedding, so Sallie volunteered to take care of them. She had been such a Godsend to them. Since she never had any children of her own, she really enjoyed caring for the babies.

Harley and his parents, Sean and Madelyn Brock, along with the Groomsmen, Mike and Pete, arrived on Friday. They seemed excited about the wedding and were happy to meet Caycee's family. Harley's Dad seemed very tired from the trip, so Miranda asked if he would like to rest awhile, which he kindly accepted. She took him upstairs to the bedroom he would be sharing with his wife. He graciously thanked her and she returned downstairs while he rested.

Madelyn Brock was a small, energetic lady. She was so excited about the wedding and talked a mile a minute. She also seemed a little nervous, which probably was the cause of her constant chatter. She informed the girls she was available to help them in any way she could. They thanked her and promised to let her know if they needed her. Jennifer and Miranda liked her from the moment they met. Jennifer could see a lot of her in her son, Harley. He was such a sweet, good natured guy. Caycee would be lucky to have him for a husband!

Everyone had such a good time last night at the rehearsal dinner. There was plenty of barbecue and the trimmings. The rehearsal went well and everyone was prepared for the wedding today. Gabe and Mardi were up early putting the final touches on the wedding site in the back yard. Huge trees surrounded the house and you could see the magnificent horses grazing in the pasture. Beautiful rainbow color flowers were surrounding a lighted arbor. It was just the perfect place to say, "I do."

Jennifer and Miranda were busy finalizing details that couldn't be done ahead of time. Ethel, Emily and Sallie also arrived early, with the wedding cake and all kinds of delicious looking food. This was going to be a wedding they wouldn't forget. Money was no object since Caycee was a fashion designer. She spared no expense. She wanted the wedding of a lifetime.

Emily and Ethel were outside setting up the crystal punch bowl, plates, cups and serving dishes. The food would be carried out later. Each table was covered with a beautiful snow white lace tablecloth. Silver trays graced the tables along with the silver cake serving set. Each table was adorned with a beautiful arrangement of rainbow colored flowers.

It was a perfect day for a wedding. The sun was shining brightly and the blue sky was clear with very few white puffy clouds. The temperature was around eighty degrees. It was just the kind of weather one would hope for on such a special occasion. The birds in the trees were singing as if they knew this was a special day. Everything seemed so perfect...

It was almost two o'clock and the wedding was about to begin. The wedding party was in place and each one proceeded to the entrance of the back door and took their place. One by one, they walked down the white carpet and took their place near the lighted arbor. Isabelle walked down the aisle scattering rose petals as she went. She took her place beside the Bridesmaids. Grayson III followed her, bearing imitation rings on a small white satin pillow. He took his place beside the Groomsmen.

The big moment was here...All eyes were fixed on the

Bride as she came walking down the aisle on the arm of Gabe. She was breathtakingly beautiful! Her long blonde hair looked like gold with the sparkling sun shining upon her head. Her twenty-five thousand dollar gown was a sight to behold. She looked like a Fairytale Princess! Harley's eyes were glued on her from the moment he first saw her. The smile of happiness that crossed his face was priceless. Caycee walked slowly, never taking her eyes off Harley until she was at the front, standing beside him. There was magic in the air. Everyone must be feeling it, as a smile graced all their faces. This long awaited day was going to be one they would never forget.

Pastor Kane Morgan, from the Laurel Baptist Church was officiating at the wedding ceremony. He was the pastor where all of them went to church. Since Caycee didn't know a minister she asked Jennifer to find one for her. He had brought his wife, Melissa, with him.

Pastor Morgan started the ceremony and there was not a sound, except for the singing of the birds. This made it even more special, thought Jennifer. She and Miranda were beautiful in their lavender dresses. Isabelle looked stunning, as well as the Maid of Honor, Jodee Williams.

"I believe Caycee and Harley have written their own vows. At this time, we will listen to what Harley has to say to his beautiful Bride," said Pastor Morgan.

"Caycee, I hardly know where to begin," said Harley with a glow on his face. "When I saw you walk down the stairs in that long red dress, I was smitten. I knew at that moment, I would marry you, that is, if you would have me. It took a little persuading for you to realize that I was the one for you. Caycee, I will be good to you and take the best of care of you as long as there is life in my body. I will never be unfaithful to you or hurt you in any way. Caycee Canfield, I will love you forever! Tears were running down his face...

"It's your turn, Caycee," said Pastor Morgan.

"Well, Harley...I feel like I'm the luckiest girl in the world. Not only did I find the Lord after finding my cousins, but through them I found the most wonderful man in the world who is about to become my husband. I am so glad you never gave up on me and made me realize what a nice guy you really are," she said with a chuckle. "There will never be another man in my life...you are my one and only. I know God has blessed me beyond any reasonable measure. I honestly don't think He would have brought you into my life if I hadn't accepted Him as my Savior. Everything works out to the good of those who love Him. So, Harley, on our Wedding Day, I just want you to know that I love you with all my heart...now and forever!"

Now they both were crying tears of joy. Pastor Morgan finished the ceremony and pronounced them Husband and Wife. Harley could hardly wait for the 'Now you may kiss your bride' part. He planted a big kiss on Caycee and held it. The crowd began to laugh. He finally let her go and they proceeded to walk back up the white carpet. Bird seed was flying through the air and covering them like snow. Lots of seeds were falling upon the ground. The birds would be very happy about this, as they too, could have a celebration.

Everyone maneuvered over to the large tent where the food was waiting. Ethel and Emily had outdone themselves. A line was formed with the Bride and Groom in the front. Each one filled their plate with delicious food and found a place to sit down.

The guests mingled and talked after eating. About an hour later, Caycee and Harley left the crowd and went into the house to change clothes. They were anxious for the horse and carriage ride that Mardi had promised them.

Mardi went into the house and changed his clothes also. He came back out wearing jeans and a plaid western shirt. He went to the barn and hooked up a couple horses to the carriage. He had promised this to Caycee and he intended to keep his promise. He drove the carriage back to the house and picked up the Bride and Groom. They started on their journey. Just as he had promised, he took them along the creek where beautiful wildflowers were in bloom. They had gotten about a mile from the barn when suddenly the horses were startled by something. Mardi caught a glimpse of two rattlesnakes stretched out in the path sunning. Upon the horses approach, the snakes woke up and reared up toward the horses, as their rattles made that dreaded sound. The spooked horses reared up in the air and dropped off the creek bank edge when they came back down. This over balanced the carriage causing it to turn over in the creek. Mardi was thrown out and landed in the creek, where he hit the top of his head on a big rock. Blood was pouring from the wound. He just lay there, still and lifeless.

When Caycee and Harley were able to get up out of the carriage they rushed over to see how bad Mardi was hurt. They weren't concerned about the bruises and minor cuts they had. "This doesn't look good," said Harley looking down at Mardi. "We need to go for help. You stay here with him while I go for help." Of all times not to have a cell phone with them.

"Okay," said Caycee. "I will try to stop the bleeding by applying direct pressure."

"Good girl. I'll be back with help as soon as I can."

Meanwhile, Caycee stayed with Mardi. She had torn off part of her skirt and wrapped around his head, while applying pressure to the wound. She prayed as she sat there waiting. It seemed like an hour, but it was only twenty minutes until she heard the sound of the Jeep. She had never been so glad to hear that sound. Almost before it stopped, Jennifer and Miranda jumped out and ran over to them. Gabe and Harley followed.

"Let me in here," demanded a stern Jennifer as she stepped forward while opening her medical bag. Caycee got up and moved out of Jennifer's way. She took out her stethoscope and listened to his lungs and heart. She then checked his pulse. "This doesn't look good at all," said Jennifer. I think he has a fractured skull and bleeding on the brain. He is unconscious and has a bloody fluid draining from his mouth and nose. His blood pressure has dropped and he is very weak. The EMT should be here soon. We have to get him to the hospital ASAP."

Miranda was crying uncontrollably. "Is he going to die?" she screamed at Jennifer.

"I don't know, Miranda. It's too soon to tell. We'll know more after he sees a neurosurgeon. He could have fragments of bone in his brain from the fracture."

"Oh, no..." she wailed as she flung her body down on his. "I can't lose you, Mardi! I just can't lose you! You are my everything! I can't make it without you! I need you... our daughter needs you! Please come back to us!!!"

"We need to PRAY, PRAY, PRAY!" exclaimed Jennifer.

The EMT arrived several minutes later. They checked his vitals and put an oxygen mask on his face. They carefully lifted Mardi onto the stretcher and loaded him into the vehicle and left. They were taking him to the Billings Medical Hospital.

Miranda, Jennifer, Gabe, Harley and Caycee hurried back to the house and told everyone what had happened. Sallie told them to go and she would stay and watch all the children. Jennifer thanked her, as she wondered what they would do without Sallie. They got into Jennifer's vehicle and rushed to the hospital. They arrived shortly after the ambulance. After inquiring about Mardi, they were told he had been taken straight to surgery. There was nothing they could do but wait and pray, which they were all doing. Jennifer was so worried about Miranda, too. This was taking a toll on her. She was not sure Miranda could make it through another death. Losing their dad almost did her in. She was praying so hard for both of them. She was also asking for God's will to be done.

Three hours later, the doctor entered the waiting room with a grim look on his face. He went straight to Miranda and said, "Mrs. Carson, I am so sorry but your husband didn't make it. We just couldn't save him."

Miranda never said a word but crumpled onto the floor. She was completely unconscious. The doctor called for help and they came and took her to the ER. Jennifer went with them.

Gabe, Harley and Caycee continued to wait and pray. Caycee was crying…"It's entirely my fault! If I hadn't asked Mardi to take us for that ride, he would be alive!"

"Don't blame yourself," said Gabe. "It's just one of those things that was destined to happen. It was Mardi's time to go. We know where he is and that is a great comfort."

"I know…but I feel so guilty!" she exclaimed wiping the tears from her eyes.

"I can understand that but you must not blame yourself. Lord knows, we will all miss Mardi but God has plans for him. We must not question God either."

"What will Miranda do? She is so torn up! I just hope she will forgive me!"

"I don't think Miranda will hold you responsible for the accident. It just happened. This will be very hard on her but we will all have to be there for her and let her know we love her and that she is not alone. She is fragile anyway and we have to be extra careful with her. She had a really hard time after her dad, Grayson, died. Thank God she has little Taylor Lynn!"

"I know but I feel sorry for the baby who will grow up without her Daddy!"

"At least she has a Mommy who loves her very much and Jennifer and I will be here for her too!" exclaimed Gabe.

"It's good that you all live in the same house," stated Caycee.

"Yes, that will help both Miranda and Taylor."

Jennifer walked into the waiting room an hour later. "Miranda woke up, but they've given her a sedative to help her relax. She will be in and out. It's best if we let her sleep." Jennifer looked at Gabe and said, "You and I will have to make the funeral arrangements. I told them to take him to Laurel Funeral Home. We will go there tomorrow and finalize everything."

"We will certainly do that for Miranda and...Mardi!" exclaimed Gabe.

"It's best if we go home for awhile and get things settled. I'm sure all the guests are gone by now. I know the family is anxiously waiting to hear the news. We need to relieve Sallie and get the children fed and ready for bed. I also told the nurses to call me if Miranda wants me. We have an ole married couple who needs to be getting on with their honeymoon, too!" she said with a smile.

"Oh, don't worry about us!" exclaimed Caycee. "We're

not going anywhere yet. We are staying for the funeral. That's the least we can do."

"How thoughtful!" exclaimed Jennifer. "I'm sure Miranda will appreciate it and so would Mardi, if he could know!"

They left the hospital and headed for the ranch. Everyone was gone except the family and Sallie. She had already fed and bathed the children and they were dressed in their pajamas.

"Oh, Sallie, you are the best!" exclaimed Jennifer. "I really do appreciate all you have done. It sure helped me out. What would I do without you? You are a Godsend to us. I am very tired, but I know I won't sleep."

"I'm happy to help. I knew you would be tired and I wanted to help you all I could. I am so sorry for all that has happened." Jennifer had called earlier and told her about Mardi's death.

"I sure hope Miranda is going to be okay!"

"I think she will, but it is going to take time. I hope she doesn't slip back into depression like she did when our Dad died, but I wouldn't be surprised if that happens. Please help us pray, Sallie!"

"Oh, I will do that for sure! Do you want me to stay the night?"

"No, you go on home and get some rest. I know you are worn out. I'm sure we will need you during the next few days. In fact, can you come over in the morning? Gabe and I are going to the funeral home at eleven o'clock to make the funeral arrangements for Mardi."

"Sure I will be here. Is ten thirty okay?"

"That will be fine and thanks again!"

"You're welcome," replied Sallie as she walked out the door.

Chapter 25

Sallie was there a few minutes before ten-thirty. She was so dependable. Gabe and Jennifer left as soon as she got there. There was little conversation on the way to the funeral home. Each one seemed to be in deep thought. Jennifer couldn't believe they were doing this. Mardi was supposed to grow old with Miranda, but God had other plans for him.

They arrived at Laurel Funeral Home a few minutes early, but the owner was waiting on them. He took them into the same room where they had made arrangements for Isac, Rachel and Grayson. Tears welled up in Jennifer's eyes. She was reliving the death of her little son and her parents. The owner, Mr. Evan Robinson, was a very nice and kind gentleman. He noticed that Jennifer was crying and tried to console her.

After getting the information he needed, Mr. Robinson led them to another room which contained the caskets. Jennifer started crying even harder. Gabe put his arms around her and held her tightly. Words were not necessary. He was feeling the same grief she was, but knew he had to be strong for her. He was glad Miranda wasn't here. He wasn't sure she could make it through this. They chose a nice cherry wood casket, similar to the ones they had chosen for their other loved ones. After everything was taken care of, they thanked Mr. Robinson and left.

They drove into Billings to see Miranda. She seemed to be some better but couldn't talk without crying. "I want to go home," she said.

"I'm sure you will be going soon. Did the doctor tell you when you can go?" asked Jennifer.

"He said I might go tomorrow. Don't have the funeral until I go home! I just have to be there for Mardi!" she exclaimed.

"Oh, we won't, Miranda. Don't worry...we'll make sure you are there," added Jennifer.

"Okay. How's Taylor?"

"She's fine," said Jennifer. "Sallie is taking good care of all the children. She is a blessing to us."

"I know," replied Miranda.

They stayed an hour with Miranda and as they were leaving, Jennifer said, "Call me in the morning when the doctor releases you and I'll come pick you up."

"Okay, I have to go to the funeral home," said Miranda.

"Gabe and I made all the arrangements for you this morning. The funeral will be on Wednesday."

"Oh, thank you so much! That made it easier for me. I love you and appreciate you very much!"

"I know. We love you, too!"

They said their good-byes and left. On the ride home, Jennifer spoke up, "I thought Miranda looked fragile. What do you think?"

"Yes, I noticed it, too. It will take time for her to get over this. I am afraid it will be much harder for her than losing her Dad."

"I think you're right, Gabe. We just have to help her all we can and be there for her."

"Of course, we will. You know, we're all family!"

They arrived home and the rest of the family was

anxious to hear the details about Miranda's condition. They were all so worried about her. Jennifer explained her condition to them and Gabe gave them the update on the funeral arrangements. Of course all of them would be staying for the funeral. Jordan and Haley went home after finding out the details. They would be back Tuesday for the viewing.

The house was mostly silent the next few days. All of them seemed to be tiptoeing around the issue of Mardi's death. It was as if it hadn't happened and everything was normal. Deep inside all of them were feeling the pain of losing Mardi but no one seemed to know what to say. So it was easier to keep silent. Even Miranda wasn't talking much about it. She seemed to be in another world. She hardly came out of her room after getting out of the hospital. She even skipped most of the meals Jennifer prepared. Somehow she could deal with Mardi's death better if she was alone. Sallie stayed on to care for the children. Miranda paid little attention to Taylor. Jennifer knew this was not good. She was really worried about her sister.

After two days without eating, Jennifer knew she had to have a serious talk with Miranda. She took a tray of food and went upstairs to her bedroom. She knocked on the door, but there was no answer. She knocked a little louder the second time. A weak voice called out, "Who is it?"

"It's Jennifer. May I come in?"

"Yes," replied Miranda.

Jennifer opened the door and set the tray on the dresser. She walked over to the window and opened the blinds. "You need to let some light in the room," she said. "I brought your dinner."

"I don't feel like eating. All I want to do is sleep."

"You need to eat, Miranda! You haven't eaten for two days. You can't gain your strength back if you don't eat!"

"I'm not sure I want to live. Everything I love has been taken from me! I lost Mom, Dad and now Mardi."

"MIRANDA!!!" scolded Jennifer. "What about little Taylor? She needs you now more than ever!"

"I love Taylor so much but I'm not sure I have the strength to take care of her any longer. You and Gabe can raise her with Isabelle and Rachel Rose. They would be like sisters."

"I can't believe I'm hearing this!" exclaimed Jennifer loudly. "You are not going to give up!!! You have to be strong for your daughter! She needs you so much! Mardi wouldn't want you to give up. He would want you to go on living and raise your daughter."

"I don't think I'm strong enough," she replied.

"Gabe and I will be here to help you. You will not be alone, not ever!"

"I just don't know, Jennifer. I feel so alone right now."

"I can understand that, Miranda but you are not alone. You have your family and we all love you very much. You know that!"

The next few days were a blur. Getting through the funeral wasn't easy. Miranda was so weak and frail. It was all she could do to stand up. Jennifer never left her side all during the funeral. She was the rock Miranda needed to lean on. Jennifer knew what she had to do after all this was over. She had to contact Miranda's doctor and make an appointment for her. Dr. Garth Sable had helped her get over the nightmares she had when their Dad died and he could help her now. Jennifer knew God would take care of her sister.

After the funeral they gathered once again at the

Parker Family Cemetery located on the ranch. The cemetery seemed to be filling up quickly, much more quickly than the family had hoped for. They knew God was in control and He knew when He needed to take each one home to be with Him. Each of us has an appointed time to go. The most important thing is to be ready to go. Jennifer knew Mardi was ready and she had no concern there. She was just concerned about helping Miranda deal with his death.

Jennifer was so deep in thought that she barely heard the Minister in his closing prayer. Miranda was sitting there with her eyes closed. The service was over and Jennifer quietly nudged her. They got up and walked out from under the tent. They had only taken a few steps when something caught their eye. They both saw it at the same time. Off to the left about fifty yards away, stood a tall, dark stranger. He was dressed in a black suit, had black hair and was wearing dark glasses. Just as Jennifer and Miranda spotted him, he swiftly turned and disappeared out of sight.

Miranda turned to Jennifer and asked in suspense, "Who was that?"

"I don't have a clue! That was weird. I've never seen him before."

"Me, neither. I wonder what he was doing here?"

"I just don't know!" replied Jennifer. "He left so quickly that we never had a chance to speak to him. I wonder if anyone else saw him."

"It was like he didn't want us to see him," added Miranda staring straight ahead.

"I guess that's another mystery that will never be solved."

"You never know. Sometime he may come back," said Miranda.

"Do you think you would recognize him again?"

"Yes, I think I would. There was something about him that makes me think I would know him if he ever crossed my path again."

"What was it?"

"I honestly don't know," said Miranda with a faraway look in her eyes.

"Let's not mention this to anyone," said Jennifer.

"I think that's a good idea!"

So they walked to the car, got in and vowed never to speak of this again. They drove back to the house in silence.

About The Author

Sally Campbell Repass is a devoted wife, mother, grandmother and great-grandmother. She has been married to her loving husband, Paul, for 10 years. They are going through a very difficult time now, as he battles Stage IV Colon cancer. Their faith in God, the love of family and dear friends, has helped ease the pain.

Sally wrote and published a Children's Fairytale Book, 'PRINCESS KARI & THE GOLDEN HAIRED BOY' in early 2010. This book was inspired by her granddaughters, Katie and Campbell.

Later that year, she published her first Inspirational Romance Book, 'FOR THE LOVE OF RACHEL'.

In 2011 she followed with a sequel, 'RACHEL'S DAUGHTER'. Not being able to let go of the family she had created, she decided to write a third book. In 2012, 'FROM THE RANCH...TO THE ISLAND' was born.

Now her fourth book in the series has been published. 'BACK HOME TO MONTANA' is the continuing saga of the Parker/Sterling families.

Look for a turn of events as the story continues in book #5.

Book #6 will be the final one in this series. As the book ends, so will the saga of this family she has grown to love. She has spanned 4 generations of the Parker/Sterling families and hopes you have enjoyed the journey as much as she has.

Website: www.fortheloveofrachel.com
Email: virginiawriter2010@gmail.com
              screpass2008@yahoo.com